ONE-COURSE MEALS

CHARMAINE SOLOMON

HAMLYN

Published 1993 by Hamlyn
an imprint of the Octopus Publishing Group,
a division of Reed International Books Australia Pty Ltd
22 Salmon Street, Port Melbourne, Victoria 3207

Designed by Louise Lavarack
Photographs by Rodney Weidland
Styling by Margaret Alcock
Food cooked by Jill Pavey, Nina Harris, Virginia McLeod
China: 'Manoir' and Medici plate by Villeroy & Boch
Ceramic bowls from Made in Japan, Neutral Bay, NSW
Typeset in 9½ on 12pt Berkeley Old Style Book by Midland Typesetters
Produced in Hong Kong by Mandarin Offset

National Library of Australia
    cataloguing-in-publication data:

Solomon, Charmaine.
    One-course meals.

    Includes index.
    ISBN 0 947334 44 0.

    1. Cookery, Oriental. 1. Title. (Series: Solomon,
    Charmaine. Asian cooking library).

641.595

INTRODUCTION

One-course meals can range from simple family fare to a veritable banquet. One thing they have in common is that no one has to clear the table and bring on another course—everything you need is right there.

One-course Meals takes you through Asia, savouring the wealth of flavours peculiar to each country and tasting some of the more famous and also lesser known dishes. Here is a great opportunity to enjoy delicious, easy-to-serve, one-course meals.

Useful Spice Formulas

While there are many different components which give delightful complexity and depth to the flavours of a dish, only a tiny amount of each is required. I suggest making spice mixes to avoid the tedium of measuring many small quantities for each recipe. It is much better to make up, for instance, four times the quantity and store it in an airtight jar. Label each mixture clearly and store it out of the sunlight. The freezer is the best place for keeping spices at optimum freshness. To ensure even distribution shake or stir before measuring out the amount required.

Whole Spice Mix
- 5 pods cardamom, bruised
- 4 whole cloves
- 1 x 8 cm (3 inch) stick cinnamon

Ground Spices I
- 2 teaspoons ground coriander
- 2 teaspoons ground cummin
- 1 teaspoon ground turmeric
- 1 teaspoon ground pepper
- 1 teaspoon chilli powder

Ground Spices II
- 2 teaspoons ground coriander
- 1 teaspoon ground cummin
- 1 teaspoon ground turmeric
- ½ teaspoon ground fennel
- ½ teaspoon ground cinnamon
- ½ teaspoon ground black pepper
- ½ teaspoon ground nutmeg
- ¼ teaspoon ground cloves
- ¼ teaspoon ground cardamom

Fragrant Ground Spices
- 1 teaspoon ground cardamom
- ½ teaspoon ground cinnamon
- ½ teaspoon ground nutmeg
- ¼ teaspoon ground cloves

INDIA

A dish for special occasions, enriched with nuts and cream, perfumed with aromatic spices and, if you want to be really impressive, decorated with silver leaf. Make it beforehand and reheat in the oven when required.

LAYERED RICE AND LAMB
Serves 10 to 12

LAMB
- 2 kg (4 lb) lean, boneless lamb
- 2 medium onions, roughly chopped
- 1 tablespoon chopped fresh ginger
- 4 cloves garlic, chopped
- 1 or 2 fresh red chillies, seeded
- 3 tablespoons ground almonds
- 3 teaspoons ground cummin
- 1 tablespoon ghee
- 2 tablespoons oil
- 2 teaspoons Fragrant Ground Spices (see p. iv)
- 2 teaspoons salt or to taste
- ½ cup yoghurt

RICE
- 1 kg (2 lb) basmati rice or other long grain rice
- 3 teaspoons salt or to taste
- 2 quantities Whole Spice Mix (see p. iv)
- 1 teaspoon saffron strands

- 1 cup cream
- 2 teaspoons kalonji (nigella) seeds

GARNISH
- ½ cup slivered almonds, fried or toasted
- ½ cup sultanas
- silver leaf, optional (see Note)

LAMB Cut lamb into cubes. Purée onion, ginger, garlic and chilli in a blender, adding a little water if needed. Add ground almonds, cummin and Fragrant Ground Spices and blend again. Fry blended mixture in ghee and oil over medium heat, stirring constantly, until cooked and aromatic—the oil should start to separate out. Add salt and lamb, turning until coated with spices. Cover and simmer until lamb is almost tender. Beat yoghurt with a little water until smooth. Stir in and cook until lamb is very tender and gravy is thick.

RICE Wash rice and soak in cold water for 30 minutes. Drain well. Place rice in a heavy pan with tight-fitting lid; add 8 cups water, salt and Whole Spice Mix. Bring quickly to boil, cover, turn heat low, and cook for 15 minutes without lifting lid. Water should be absorbed and rice almost cooked. Toast saffron strands in a small, heavy pan for a few seconds—don't let them burn. Crush to powder, dissolve in ¼ cup boiling water and stir into cream.

Grease a large, heavy casserole with extra ghee or oil and spread evenly with half the rice. Pour half the cream over. Sprinkle with half the kalonji seeds. Cover with cooked lamb mixture, spreading to the edges. Spread remaining rice over lamb and pour remaining cream over; sprinkle with remaining kalonji seeds. Press down with a square of buttered foil.

To prevent rice drying out during baking, sprinkle 2 to 3 tablespoons of water on top of foil before covering with lid. Bake in an oven preheated to 160°C (325°F) for about 40 minutes. Serve in casserole, garnished with almonds, sultanas and silver leaf.

Note This pure silver leaf is very delicate and difficult to handle, so make sure your fingers are dry. Hold the thin sheets of tissue in which it is packed and allow the silver to flutter gently onto the rice in a few different spots.

An excellent one-dish meal for vegetarians. Accompany it with peeled and diced tomatoes, dressed with a pinch of chilli powder and salt, a bowl of yoghurt and some Indian pickles or chutneys.

RICE WITH LENTILS
Serves 4 to 6

- 1 cup moong dhal (skinned, split moong beans)
- ½ cup red lentils
- 500 g (1 lb) basmati or other long grain rice
- 500 g (1 lb) fresh peas
- 1 tablespoon ghee
- 2 tablespoons vegetable oil
- 1 quantity Whole Spice Mix (see p. iv)
- 4 large onions, finely sliced
- 1 tablespoon finely grated fresh ginger
- 1 fresh green chilli, seeded and sliced
- ½ teaspoon cummin seeds
- ½ teaspoon ground turmeric
- 1 teaspoon ground cummin
- 5 cups hot water
- 2 teaspoons salt, or to taste
- 2 tablespoons chopped fresh coriander leaves

Roast moong dhal in a dry pan, stirring constantly, until golden brown. Transfer to a bowl, wash well, then drain and set aside. Wash red lentils separately and leave to drain. If using basmati

3

rice or any other which needs washing, wash well and set aside to drain for 30 minutes. Shell peas.

Heat ghee and oil in a heavy saucepan. Add Whole Spice Mix and sliced onions. Fry over medium heat, stirring frequently, until onions are golden brown. Transfer onions to a plate with a slotted spoon, leaving whole spices.

Add ginger, chilli and cummin seeds to oil left in pan. Fry, stirring, until ginger is golden. Add rice and red lentils and fry, stirring, for 3 minutes. Add turmeric and ground cummin; fry for 30 seconds before adding peas, moong dhal, water and salt and bring to boil. Turn heat very low. Cover and cook for 30 to 35 minutes, or until liquid is absorbed and peas tender. Transfer to a serving dish with a slotted metal spoon. Garnish with fried onions and chopped coriander.

Known as Dhansak this filling dish is a Sunday favourite with Parsi families in India. It makes a complete meal when served with rice and accompaniments. Do not be daunted by the number of ingredients: just prepare each section separately and combine.

CHICKEN OR LAMB WITH LENTILS
Serves 8 to 10

LENTILS
- *1 cup yellow split peas*
- *½ cup moong dhal*
- *½ cup red lentils*

VEGETABLES
- *250 g (8 oz) piece of pumpkin*
- *1 large potato*
- *2 medium onions*
- *2 ripe tomatoes*
- *1 medium eggplant*
- *2 cups spinach leaves*
- *small bunch fresh fenugreek leaves*
or 1 tablespoon dried fenugreek leaves, optional

Meat
- *1 x 2 kg (4 lb) chicken or 1.5 kg (3 lb) leg lamb, boned*
- *salt to taste*

Fresh Masala
- *6 red chillies, seeded*
- *6 fresh green chillies, seeded*
- *1 tablespoon chopped fresh ginger*
- *10 cloves garlic, peeled*
- *½ cup fresh mint leaves*
- *½ cup fresh coriander leaves*

Dry Ground Masala
- *3 tablespoons Ground Spices II (see p. iv)*
- *½ teaspoon black mustard seeds, lightly crushed*
- *¼ teaspoon ground fenugreek seeds*

For Cooking
- *3 to 4 tablespoons ghee*
- *4 medium onions, finely sliced*

Wash all lentils and soak overnight in water to cover. Peel and roughly chop pumpkin, potato, onions and tomatoes. Wash eggplant, spinach and fenugreek leaves; chop roughly.

Joint chicken, or chop lamb into large cubes. Place in a large saucepan with drained lentils. Add sufficient water to cover. Add salt to taste, cover and simmer for 15 minutes. Add chopped vegetables and continue to cook until chicken or lamb is almost tender. Remove pieces of chicken or lamb and set aside. Purée lentils and vegetables.

Blend ingredients for Fresh Masala to a smooth purée with ¼ cup hot water. Combine ingredients for Dry Ground Masala.

Fry onions in hot ghee in a large saucepan, stirring frequently, until onions are browned. Remove with a slotted spoon. Add Fresh and Dry Masalas to pan. Fry, stirring constantly, until aromatic. Add cooked chicken or lamb, lentil and vegetable purée and half of browned onions. Simmer for 20 to 30 minutes. Add salt to taste if necessary. Garnish with remaining fried onions.

A simple, satisfying meal with flat bread or rice.

Eggs with Savoury Mince
Serves 4

- 2 tablespoons ghee or oil
- 1 large onion, finely chopped
- 2 fresh green chillies, seeded and chopped
- 2 small cloves garlic, finely chopped
- 1 teaspoon finely chopped ginger
- 1½ tablespoons Ground Spices I (see p. iv)
- 750 g (1½ lb) minced lamb or beef
- 1 ripe tomato, peeled and chopped
- salt to taste
- 1 teaspoon garam masala
- 4 tablespoons finely chopped fresh coriander
- 4 eggs
- black pepper to taste

Heat ghee or oil in a pan and fry onion, chillies, garlic and ginger until golden, stirring frequently. Add Ground Spices I and cook, stirring for 1 minute, then add meat and fry, stirring until it changes colour. Add tomato, salt and ½ cup water. Cover and cook until meat is tender and liquid almost absorbed. Sprinkle with garam masala and mix in with half of chopped coriander. Spread meat mixture in a greased ovenproof dish. Make 4 depressions in surface with back of a spoon and break an egg into each.

Bake in oven preheated to 190°C (375°F) until eggs are set. Sprinkle with remaining fresh coriander. Serve immediately, with black pepper for seasoning eggs.

A festive dish for special occasions. Chicken is cooked in a spicy sauce, then layered with a pilau rice. Halve the quantity for a family meal. Accompany with fresh chutney, raita (cooling salad with yoghurt) and hot Indian pickle.

MOGUL-STYLE SPICED RICE WITH CHICKEN
Serves 10 to 12

- 12 chicken thigh cutlets or drumsticks
- 10 small new potatoes
- 3 tablespoons ghee
- 3 tablespoons oil
- 4 large onions, finely chopped
- 4 cloves garlic, finely chopped
- 1 tablespoon finely grated fresh ginger
- 1½ tablespoons Ground Spices I (see p. iv)
- 2 teaspoons salt, or to taste
- 3 large ripe tomatoes, peeled and chopped
- 1 cup yoghurt
- ¼ cup chopped fresh mint
- 2 fresh red chillies
- 1 teaspoon ground cardamom
- 1 small cinnamon stick

PILAU RICE
- 1 kg (2 lb) basmati or other long grain rice
- 3 tablespoons ghee

- 1 teaspoon saffron strands
- 2 quantities Whole Spice Mix (see p. iv)
- 1 teaspoon ground lesser galangal
- salt to taste
- 8 cups hot chicken stock

GARNISH
- 2 large, finely sliced onions, fried
- ½ cup sultanas, fried
- ½ cup slivered almonds, toasted
- 8 hard boiled eggs, halved
- 1 cup cooked green peas

Trim excess fat from chicken thighs. Peel potatoes and cut into halves. Heat ghee and oil together in a small frying pan. Fry potatoes until outer surface is browned, remove and set aside.

Pour ghee and oil remaining in pan into a large saucepan. Add onions, garlic and ginger; stirring frequently, until soft and golden. Add Ground Spices, salt and tomatoes. Fry, stirring constantly, for 5 minutes. Stir in yoghurt, mint, whole chillies, cardamom and cinnamon. Cover and cook over low heat, stirring occasionally, until tomato is cooked to a pulp—add a little hot water if mixture starts to stick.

When tomato mixture is thick add chicken pieces, turn in mixture to coat. Cover and cook over very low heat until chicken is tender—about 40 minutes. There should be only a small amount of sauce left—if there is too much liquid, uncover pan for the last 10 to 15 minutes of cooking time to allow evaporation.

PILAU RICE   Wash rice well and drain in sieve for at least 30 minutes. Heat saffron strands for a few seconds on a dry pan—do not let them burn. Crush and dissolve in 1 tablespoon hot water. Heat ghee in saucepan, add dissolved saffron, Whole Spice Mix, galangal and rice. Stir constantly until rice is coated with ghee. Add salt to chicken stock and stir into rice. Gently mix in cooked chicken and potatoes. Cover pan tightly and cook mixture over very low heat for 25 minutes. Do not lift lid until end of cooking time, then uncover and allow steam to escape for a few minutes.

Use a metal spoon to transfer chicken and rice mixture to a serving dish; Garnish and serve.

As vegetables are included in this curry you will only need plain rice, raita or chutneys and pickles to complete the meal.

MASALA KING PRAWNS
Serves 4 to 6

- 750 g (1½ lb) raw king prawns
- 8 dried red chillies
- 2 teaspoons chopped fresh ginger
- 2 teaspoons chopped garlic
- ½ teaspoon ground cinnamon
- 2 teaspoons Ground Spices I
- ¼ cup vinegar
- 4 tablespoons oil
- 3 medium onions, finely sliced
- 1 green capsicum, finely sliced
- 1 red capsicum, finely sliced
- 3 ripe tomatoes, peeled and chopped
- salt to taste

Wash prawns and drain, but do not remove shells or heads. Soak chillies in hot water for 5 minutes. Place ginger, garlic, chillies into a blender and blend to a smooth paste with Ground Spices and vinegar.

Heat 2 tablespoons of the oil and fry sliced vegetables until soft, stirring. Add prawns and stir-fry over high heat, just until they change colour. Remove to a plate. Heat remaining oil and fry blended spices on low heat for about 5 minutes, stirring. Add tomatoes and salt. Simmer, covered, for 10 minutes. Return prawns and vegetables and simmer 10 minutes longer.

Serve this aromatic curry with rice, or Indian bread and fresh chutney.

SPINACH AND LAMB CURRY
Serves 4

- *500 g (1 lb) boneless lamb or mutton*
- *1 large bunch spinach*
- *1 large onion, roughly chopped*
- *1 tablespoon chopped fresh ginger*
- *2 large cloves garlic, chopped*
- *4 dried red chillies*
- *3 tablespoons oil or ghee*
- *½ teaspoon kalonji (nigella) seeds*
- *salt to taste*
- *5 cardamom pods, bruised*
- *½ cup plain yoghurt*
- *¼ teaspoon ground black pepper*

Trim off any fat and cut meat into cubes. Wash spinach well and chop roughly. Purée onion, ginger, garlic and chillies (broken into pieces) in a blender, adding a little water if necessary.

Heat oil or ghee in a heavy saucepan and fry kalonji seeds for 1 minute. Add blended mixture and fry, stirring, until it browns and oil starts to separate from mixture—about 10 minutes. Stir in meat until cubes are well coated. Cover and cook on low heat until juices come out of meat. Add spinach, salt and cardamom pods. Cover and cook until liquid is absorbed and meat is tender. Remove from heat, stir in yoghurt and pepper.

A colourful dish from Rajasthan. Serve with pickle and rice.

Curried Lamb with Sweet Corn
Serves 4

- 500 g (1 lb) lamb shoulder or forequarter chops
- 3 tablespoons oil or ghee
- 4 medium onions, sliced finely
- 1 medium stick cinnamon
- 4 whole cloves
- 6 black peppercorns
- 1 teaspoon finely chopped fresh ginger
- 2 cloves garlic, finely chopped
- 1 tablespoon ground coriander
- 2 large ripe tomatoes, peeled and chopped
- 2 corn cobs, cut in pieces
- salt to taste
- ½ cup plain yoghurt
- 2 teaspoons sugar
- 2 tablespoons chopped fresh coriander
- few sprigs fresh coriander
- 1 purple onion, finely sliced lengthwise
- 1 green chilli, sliced into strips
- cherry tomatoes, halved

Cut lamb into cubes, but retain bones to cook in the curry for flavour. Heat oil or ghee in a large, heavy saucepan and fry onions with the cinnamon, cloves and peppercorns, stirring occasionally. When onions are golden add ginger and garlic and continue stirring until golden brown. Stir in ground coriander, tomatoes, corn and salt to taste. Cover and cook for 5 minutes.

Stir in lamb and bring mixture to boil. Simmer for 10 minutes. Beat yoghurt until smooth and stir into curry. Cover and simmer over low heat until meat is tender, adding a little hot water if necessary to prevent mixture from sticking to pan. Stir in sugar and chopped coriander just before serving. Transfer to a serving dish and garnish with coriander leaves, sliced onion, chilli, and halved cherry tomatoes. Serve hot with rice.

A Major Grey type chutney that keeps well.

FRUIT CHUTNEY
Makes about 2½ cups

- 2 cooking apples, peeled, cored and diced
- 25 dried apricot halves
- ½ cup sultanas
- 1 tablespoon finely chopped fresh ginger
- 1 tablespoon finely sliced garlic
- 1 tablespoon chopped fresh red chillies
- 1½ cups sugar
- 1 cup cider vinegar
- 3 teaspoons sea salt
- 1 teaspoon cummin seeds
- 1 teaspoon kalonji (nigella) seeds
- 2 teaspoons garam masala

Put all ingredients in a heavy enamel or stainless steel pan. (It is best not to use aluminium pans when cooking with acids such as vinegar.) Add 1 cup water and stir over medium heat to dissolve sugar. Bring to boil, turn heat low and simmer, uncovered, for 30 minutes or until thick. Bottle.

Steamed vegetables are added to a spicy sauce and garnished with hard-boiled eggs and tomatoes. Serve with rice or parathas.

SPICY CHICKEN WITH VEGETABLES
Serves 4

- *1 x 1.5 kg (3 lb) roasting chicken or prepared chicken pieces—drumsticks, thighs or half breasts*
- *2 cloves garlic*
- *salt to taste*
- *1 teaspoon finely grated fresh ginger*
- *1 teaspoon ground cardamom*
- *½ teaspoon ground nutmeg*
- *½ teaspoon ground black pepper*
- *1 tablespoon ghee*
- *2 tablespoons oil*
- *1 fresh green chilli, seeded and chopped*
- *½ cup roasted cashews, finely chopped*
- *mixture of steamed vegetables, such as cauliflower sprigs, carrot sticks, green beans, peas*
- *2 hard-boiled eggs, quartered*
- *2 firm red tomatoes, sliced*

Cut chicken into serving pieces. Crush garlic to a smooth paste with salt. Mix with ginger and ground spices to form a paste. Rub paste over chicken pieces. Set aside for at least 30 minutes.

Heat ghee and oil in a heavy pan and brown chicken pieces, turning and stirring carefully. Add chilli and cashews; cook for 1 to 2 minutes. Stir in about ¼ cup water. Cover and simmer over low heat until chicken is cooked—about 10 minutes. Transfer chicken pieces to a serving dish. Add steamed vegetables to pan and toss in spicy sauce. Arrange on serving dish with chicken. Garnish with eggs and tomatoes.

Serve this full-flavoured omelette for lunch with flat Indian bread or readily available pita bread.

PARSI OMELETTE
Serves 2

- *1 cup diced potato*
- *2 tablespoons ghee or oil*
- *4 eggs*
- *salt and pepper to taste*
- *½ teaspoon ground cummin*
- *2 tablespoons finely chopped fresh coriander*
- *1 small onion, finely chopped*
- *2 fresh green chillies, seeded and chopped*

Parboil potato in lightly salted water and drain well. Heat half the ghee or oil in a frying pan or omelette pan and fry potato, stirring frequently over medium heat, until lightly browned. Remove with slotted spoon and set aside.

Separate eggs and beat whites until frothy, then beat in yolks, salt, pepper and cummin. Fold in coriander, onion and chillies.

Wipe out pan with paper towel. Add remaining ghee or oil and heat, swirling to coat pan. Pour in egg mixture and when it starts to set sprinkle fried potato over surface. Cook over low heat until golden brown underneath; carefully turn omelette over with a spatula and cook until browned on other side. Serve hot.

SRI LANKA

This curry has a rich, thick and spicy gravy. Serve it with Shredded Cabbage (see p. 16) and plain white rice.

BEEF CURRY
Serves 6

- 1.25 kg (2¼ lb) stewing steak
- 1 walnut-size piece of tamarind pulp
- 2 tablespoons ghee
- 2 medium onions, finely chopped
- 6 cloves garlic, finely chopped
- 1 tablespoon finely chopped fresh ginger
- 1 stick cinnamon
- sprig of fresh or 10 dried curry leaves
- 1 stalk lemon grass or 2 strips lemon rind
- 3 tablespoons Ceylon curry powder
- 1 teaspoon ground turmeric
- 1 teaspoon chilli powder
- 1½ cups canned coconut milk
- 2 teaspoons salt or to taste

Slice meat into strips. Soak tamarind in ½ cup hot water for 5 to 10 minutes, squeeze to dissolve pulp and strain, discarding seeds and fibres. Heat ghee in a large, heavy saucepan and when hot add meat in batches, stirring over high heat, until browned all over. Push meat to side of pan as it cooks.

When all meat is browned, add tamarind liquid and

remaining ingredients, reserving ½ cup of coconut milk. Add 1½ cups water and stir to mix well. Cover pan and simmer gently until meat is tender—about 1½ hours. Add reserved coconut milk and cook, uncovered, for 15 minutes more. If gravy appears too thin once meat is tender, cook over high heat, uncovered, until thickened and reduced.

SHREDDED CABBAGE
Serves 6

- *375 g (12 oz) cabbage*
- *1 large onion, finely chopped*
- *2 fresh green chillies, seeded and finely chopped*
- *½ teaspoon ground turmeric*
- *½ teaspoon freshly ground black pepper*
- *salt to taste*
- *2 teaspoons dried prawn powder*
- *¾ cup desiccated coconut*

Shred cabbage very finely. Wash, then drain and place in a large saucepan with water that clings to leaves. Add remaining ingredients except for coconut. Cover and cook over very low heat, just until cabbage is tender, stirring occasionally. Do not overcook—it should still be bright green in colour. Uncover and stir in coconut. The dish is ready when any remaining liquid has been absorbed by coconut.

This combination of vegetables and cashew nuts makes an excellent dish for vegetarians. Serve with plain rice and Fried Onion Sambal (see p. 27).

VEGETABLE AND CASHEW CURRY
Serves 4 to 6

- 1 x 400 mL can coconut milk
- 1 medium onion, finely sliced
- 2 fresh green chillies, seeded and split into halves
- ½ teaspoon ground turmeric
- 3 cloves garlic, finely sliced
- 1 teaspoon finely grated fresh ginger
- small piece cinnamon stick
- 1 stalk lemon grass
- sprig fresh curry leaves
- 125 g (4 oz) raw cashew nuts, soaked 1 hour in cold water
- 750 g (1½ lb) prepared and sliced vegetables
- salt to taste

Put 1 cup of canned coconut milk with 2 cups water in a large saucepan. Add onion, chillies, turmeric, garlic, ginger, cinnamon, lemon grass and curry leaves. Pour away soaking water and stir in cashews. Simmer over low heat, uncovered, for about 10 minutes. Add vegetables with salt to taste and cook gently until vegetables are just tender. Stir in remaining coconut milk and simmer for a further 5 minutes.

The yellow rice which forms the basis of this dish has a delicate, spicy flavour and is cooked in coconut milk. The rice is moulded into a cup over a hard-boiled egg and flavoured with coconut sambol. It is ideal for picnics (you can transport it in the cups), or you can unmould it for a light lunch or serve it with curry.

CUP RICE
Serves 4 to 6

- 500 g (1 lb) long grain rice
- 2 tablespoons ghee
- 2 medium brown onions, finely sliced
- ¼ teaspoon whole cloves
- ¼ teaspoon black peppercorns
- 1 teaspoon cardamom pods, bruised
- 1½ teaspoons ground turmeric
- 12 curry leaves
- 1 stalk lemon grass
- 1 x 400 mL can coconut milk
- 1½ teaspoons salt
- 4 hard-boiled eggs

COCONUT SAMBOL
- 1 cup desiccated coconut
- 1 teaspoon salt
- 1 teaspoon chilli powder
- 2 tablespoons dried prawns, powdered

- *1 medium onion, chopped*
  - *¼ cup lemon juice*

Wash and drain rice thoroughly. In a large saucepan, heat ghee; add onions and fry until golden brown. Add cloves, peppercorns, cardamom pods, turmeric, curry leaves and lemon grass. Stir in rice and fry, stirring constantly, for about 3 minutes, or until rice is well coated with ghee. Add coconut milk, mixed with 2½ cups water. Stir in salt and bring to boil. Lower heat, cover and cook for 20 to 25 minutes without lifting lid.

The spices will rise to the surface when rice is cooked. Remove spices and leaves; lightly fluff up rice with a fork.

Halve hard-boiled eggs crosswise and place one half, cut side upwards, in the bottom of a cup. Half-fill with warm rice and press firmly. Cover with a tablespoon of Coconut Sambol, then add more rice to fill cup, pressing down firmly again. Turn out onto a plate. Repeat with remaining ingredients until all rice is used.

COCONUT SAMBOL   Place coconut in a heavy-based frying pan and heat, stirring constantly, until it is evenly browned. Do not let it burn. Transfer to a large plate and spread out to cool. Place coconut in a blender with other ingredients and process until well mixed. Transfer to a bowl.

One of Sri Lanka's staple breakfast dishes comprises stringhoppers. What, you may ask, are stringhoppers? They are lacy, saucer-sized rounds of fine strings of dough made from rice flour and water pressed out with a special mould and steamed. They are served with Coconut Sambol (see p. 18) or with sugar and fresh grated coconut.

Leftovers are pulled into small pieces to make a spicy pilau and the resulting dish is much richer and tastier than stringhoppers served at breakfast. The easy way to make this dish is to start with rice vermicelli, eliminating the process of making stringhoppers.

RICE VERMICELLI PILAU
Serves 4 to 5

- 250 g (8 oz) rice vermicelli
- 6 slices streaky bacon, chopped
- 2 tablespoons ghee
- 2 onions, finely sliced
- 1 teaspoon ground turmeric
- 1 teaspoon ground cardamom
- salt and pepper to taste
- 4 hard-boiled eggs
- 1 cup cooked peas

Drop vermicelli into a large pan of lightly salted boiling water for 2 minutes, drain immediately. Cook bacon in ghee with onions until both are golden. Add ground spices, rice vermicelli, salt and pepper and mix thoroughly with metal spoon to distribute seasonings. Serve hot, garnished with quartered hard-boiled eggs and cooked peas.

Note   For a more substantial meal, leftover cooked chicken or meat may be sliced and added, or joints of fried chicken placed around the dish.

INDONESIA

A soup that is a meal on its own. Sambal ulek is served in a separate bowl and added to individual servings according to taste— remember that the sambal is very fiery!

CHICKEN SOUP
Serves 6 to 8

- 1 x 2 kg (4 lb) roasting chicken or chicken pieces
- 2 teaspoons salt, or to taste
- 1 teaspoon whole peppercorns
- 12 sprigs celery leaves
- 4 small onions
- 500 g (1 lb) fine egg noodles
- 3 tablespoons peanut oil
- 2 teaspoons chopped red chilli
- sprig of fresh or 10 dried curry leaves
- 4 cloves garlic, finely chopped
- 3 teaspoons finely chopped fresh ginger
- 1 teaspoon dried shrimp paste
- 4 tablespoons Ground Spices II (see p. iv)
- juice of 1 large lemon
- 250 g (8 oz) fresh bean sprouts
- 6 hard-boiled eggs, chopped
- 4 spring onions, finely sliced
- sambal ulek
- Fried Onion Flakes (see p. 22)

Joint chicken and place in a saucepan with 2.5 litres (10 cups) cold water. Add salt, peppercorns, celery leaves and 1 onion. Bring to boil, reduce heat, cover and simmer gently until chicken is tender. Cool to lukewarm, strain stock into a bowl. Remove skin and bones from chicken and cut flesh into small pieces. Set aside.

Soak noodles in warm water for 10 minutes, drain and cook in boiling water for 2 minutes. Drain in colander, run cold water through.

Slice remaining onions finely. Heat oil in a large pan and fry onion, chilli and curry leaves, stirring frequently, until onion starts to brown. Add garlic, ginger and shrimp paste; fry, crushing shrimp paste with spoon. Add Ground Spices and fry for a few seconds longer. Add strained stock and bring to boil, then reduce heat, cover and simmer for 10 minutes. Add lemon juice, noodles and chicken pieces; heat through. Taste and adjust seasonings.

Rinse bean sprouts under cold water, drain and place in a serving bowl or individual soup plates. Garnish with chopped eggs, spring onions and Fried Onion Flakes and serve immediately.

FRIED ONION FLAKES

Crisply fried sliced shallots are sold in Asian food stores, but if you cannot buy these use dried onions. To fry them, place on a wire strainer and lower into hot, deep oil (it should not be too hot, however, or the flakes will burn and taste bitter). They will only take a few seconds to turn golden brown. Lift out immediately and drain on paper towel. When cool, store in an airtight bottle and use as needed.

A popular dish combining omelette, seafood, meats and rice.

FRIED RICE
Serves 6

- 3 eggs
- salt and pepper to taste
- oil for frying
- 250 g (8 oz) raw prawns
- 250 g (8 oz) lean beef
- 2 medium onions, roughly chopped
- 2 cloves garlic
- ½ teaspoon dried shrimp paste
- 4 cups cold cooked rice
- 6 spring onions, thinly sliced
- 2 tablespoons light soy sauce
- 3 tablespoons Fried Onion Flakes (see p. 22)
- 1 green cucumber, thinly sliced

Beat eggs with salt and pepper to taste. Heat a little oil in
an omelette pan and make a thin omelette with half the beaten
eggs. Turn onto a plate to cool—do not fold. Repeat with
remaining mixture. When cool, place one omelette on top of
the other; roll up and cut across into thin strips.

Shell and devein prawns. Cut beef into very fine strips.
Put onion, garlic and shrimp paste in a blender or food
processor and blend to a paste, adding a little water if necessary.

23

Heat 2 tablespoons of oil in a wok or large frying pan and fry blended paste, stirring frequently, until cooked. Add beef and prawns to pan and stir-fry, tossing ingredients until cooked. Push to side of pan. Add 2 more tablespoons oil and when hot stir in rice and spring onions, tossing to mix. When very hot sprinkle with soy sauce and mix everything thoroughly. Serve fried rice garnished with strips of omelette, Fried Onion Flakes and cucumber slices.

Spicy Beef in Coconut Milk
Serves 6 to 8

- 1.5 kg (3 lb) blade steak
- 3 large onions, roughly chopped
- 6 large cloves garlic
- 1 tablespoon chopped ginger
- 6 fresh red chillies
- 2 tablespoons Ground Spices II (see p. iv)
- 1 teaspoon ground lesser galangal
- 1 x 560 mL can coconut milk
- 2 teaspoons salt or to taste
- 1 tablespoon dried tamarind pulp
- 1 tablespoon palm sugar

Cut beef in thick strips. Purée onions, garlic, ginger and chillies in blender or food processor with Ground Spices and galangal. Mix with 2 cups coconut milk and 3 cups water. Add salt and pour over beef in a large, heavy saucepan. Stir until boiling. Reduce heat and simmer, uncovered, for 2 hours. Soak tamarind in ½ cup hot water to soften, squeeze to dissolve pulp, strain. Add to pan, simmer until beef is tender and gravy thick. Stir in palm sugar and remaining coconut milk, simmer for 5 minutes longer. Serve with rice and Fried Onion Sambal (see p. 27), Pineapple Curry (see p. 30) or Vegetable Pickle (see p. 42).

Serve with white rice and accompaniments such as bottled sambals.

FISH WITH STIR-FRIED VEGETABLES
Serves 6

- 750 g (1½ lb) fish cutlets or steaks—use a firm fish such as jewfish, mackerel or tuna
- salt
- 2 medium onions
- 3 large, fresh red chillies
- 1 red capsicum
- 185 g (6 oz) fresh green beans
- 1 cup sliced canned bamboo shoots
- 3 cloves garlic, finely chopped
- 2 teaspoons finely grated fresh ginger
- 2 tablespoons thick bean sauce
- 2 tablespoons peanut oil
- 1 tablespoon light soy sauce

Cut fish into serving pieces. Sprinkle with salt and set aside. Peel and cut 1 onion in six wedges lengthwise, then cut each section in half across and separate layers. Remove membranes and seeds from chillies and capsicum. Cut lengthwise into strips and cut strips across in half. Trim beans and slice diagonally. Slice bamboo shoots in pieces of a similar size. Set each vegetable aside separately.

Chop remaining onion finely and mix with garlic, ginger

and bean sauce. Heat oil in wok or frying pan and fry onion mixture, stirring constantly, over medium heat until onion is soft. Add green beans and stir-fry for 2 minutes. Add chilli and capsicum strips with onion slices and stir-fry for 1 minute. Stir in bamboo shoots with soy sauce and 2/3 cup water. Dry fish on paper towels and add to pan. Bring to a simmer and cook, covered, until fish is ready.

A satisfying one-course meal of noodles, meat, prawns and crisp vegetables.

FRIED NOODLES
Serves 4

- *250 g (8 oz) fine egg noodles*
- *250 g (8 oz) boneless pork*
- *250 g (8 oz) raw prawns*
- *4 tablespoons peanut oil*
- *1 onion, finely chopped*
- *3 cloves garlic, finely chopped*
- *1 fresh red chilli, seeded and sliced*
- *½ teaspoon dried shrimp paste*
- *2 stalks celery, finely sliced*
- *2 cups finely shredded cabbage*
- *salt and black pepper to taste*
- *2 tablespoons light soy sauce*
- *Fried Onion Flakes (see p. 22)*
- *4 spring onions, sliced including green*
- *thinly sliced green cucumber*

Soak noodles in warm water while boiling a large saucepan of water. Drain noodles and drop into boiling water. When water returns to the boil, cook for 1 to 3 minutes, testing a strand about every 30 seconds—the noodles should be tender but firm to bite. Be careful not to overcook. Drain noodles in a colander as soon as they are ready and run under cold water to cool. Drain well.

Remove rind or fat from pork and cut meat into small dice. Shell and devein prawns. Heat oil in a wok or large, deep frying pan and fry onion, garlic and chilli until onion is soft and starts to turn golden. Add shrimp paste, fry 1 minute. Add pork and prawns and stir-fry, tossing until cooked. Add celery and cabbage and fry for 1 minute more. Vegetables should still be crisp. Add noodles and turn constantly until heated through. Season with salt, pepper and soy sauce.

Turn into a serving dish and sprinkle with Fried Onion Flakes and spring onions. Arrange cucumber slices around edge of dish. Serve immediately.

Sambalan is a collective term given to those highly spiced, frequently hot accompaniments served with most meals which consist mainly of rice or noodles. They cross borders with ease and compliment the food of many Asian countries.

FRIED ONION SAMBAL
Serves 4 to 6

- ½ cup oil
- 2 large onions, finely sliced
- 6 dried chillies, broken into pieces (discard seeds if you want it milder)
- 2 tablespoons prawn powder
- salt to taste
- 2 tablespoons lemon juice

Heat oil in a heavy frying pan and fry onion over low heat until soft and transparent. Add chilli pieces and prawn powder. Cover and cook, stirring occasionally, for 10 to 15 minutes—the oil will start to separate from rest of ingredients. Add salt and lemon juice and cook for a few minutes more. Transfer to a small bowl.

A restaurant favourite as a first course, this also makes a satisfying main course and is served at room temperature with plain rice.

VEGETABLES WITH PEANUT SAUCE
Serves 6

- 6 medium potatoes, boiled
- 250 g (8 oz) fresh bean sprouts
- 500 g (1 lb) green beans
- 3 carrots
- ½ small cabbage
- 1 green cucumber
- small bunch watercress
- 6 hard-boiled eggs

PEANUT SAUCE
- 8 tablespoons peanut butter
- 1 teaspoon crushed garlic
- 2 teaspoons palm sugar or dark brown sugar
- 2 tablespoons dark soy sauce
- 2 tablespoons lemon juice
- 1 teaspoon shrimp paste
- 2 tablespoons crisp fried onions
- canned coconut milk or water for thinning

Peel potatoes and cut in slices. Wash bean sprouts and pinch off straggly tails. Pour boiling water over sprouts in colander, then rinse under cold water; leave to drain. Trim beans and cut in diagonal slices. Cook in lightly salted boiling water until tender but still crisp. Scrub carrots and cut into thin strips: cook until just tender. Drain. Slice cabbage, discarding tough centre stem. Blanch briefly in boiling salted water, drain and refresh under cold water. Score skin of cucumber with a fork and cut into very thin slices. Wash watercress and break into sprigs, discarding tough stalks. Chill until crisp.

Place watercress on a large platter and arrange the various vegetables in separate sections on top. Surround with slices of cucumber and arrange wedges of hard-boiled egg in centre. Serve cold, accompanied by Peanut Sauce and plain rice. The sauce is spooned over individual servings.

PEANUT SAUCE   Place peanut butter in a saucepan with 1 cup water, stirring over gentle heat until well mixed. Remove from heat and stir in remaining ingredients. Add a little coconut milk or water to thin to a thick pouring consistency. Add more salt and lemon juice if needed.

PINEAPPLE CURRY
Serves 6 to 8

- *1 slightly under-ripe pineapple*
- *2 onions, roughly chopped*
- *4 cloves garlic, peeled*
- *3 or 4 fresh red chillies, seeded*
- *1 teaspoon shrimp paste*
- *2 teaspoons Fragrant Ground Spices (see p. iv)*
- *2 tablespoons oil*
- *1 cup canned coconut milk*
- *1 teaspoon salt or to taste*
- *2 teaspoons palm sugar or brown sugar*
- *¼ cup small fresh basil leaves*

Using a sharp stainless steel knife remove pineapple skin. With a series of diagonal cuts forming a V, remove 'eyes' three at a time. Cut pineapple in long wedges, remove core. Purée onions, garlic, chillies, shrimp paste and spices in blender. Heat oil and fry purée on low heat for 15 minutes, stirring. Add pineapple, coconut milk, salt and sugar. Stir and simmer for 5 minutes. Sprinkle with basil leaves and serve as an extra dish with rice and curries.

SINGAPORE

KNOW YOUR NOODLES

There is a multitude of noodles to choose from throughout Asia.

Fresh rice noodles are made every morning and sold by nightfall. They are cut into slices and stir-fried or used in soup.

It is not essential to use fresh noodles—their dried counterparts are just as good. Dried noodles are made from such things as rice, wheat, eggs and bean starch.

Follow cooking times and soaking instructions carefully, however, because, like well-cooked pasta, noodles should never be soggy, rather tender but firm. For instance, fresh egg noodles need only a moment in boiling water, dried rice noodles 1 minute, and dried egg noodles 2 or 3 minutes before they are drained for frying or adding to a soup or curry. Rice vermicelli, on the other hand, needs 10 minutes soaking in hot water.

Here is evidence of the strong Chinese influence in Singaporean cuisine.

Soup Noodles
Serves 4

- 500 g (1 lb) raw prawns
- 2 tablespoons peanut oil
- 5 sections star anise
- 2 cups chicken stock
- salt to taste
- 125 g (4 oz) fine egg noodles
- 250 g (8 oz) barbecued or roasted pork
- 250 g (8 oz) bean sprouts
- 3 cloves garlic, finely grated
- ½ teaspoon finely grated fresh ginger
- 200 g (7½ oz) fish cakes, sliced
- 1 teaspoon sesame oil
- ½ cup finely chopped spring onion
- ½ cup diced green cucumber

Shell and devein prawns. Wash prawn heads and shells and drain. Heat 1 tablespoon peanut oil in a wok or saucepan and fry heads and shells over high heat until they turn pink. Add 4 cups water and star anise, cover and cook for 20 minutes. Strain, reserving stock. Put prawn heads and shells in a food processor or blender with some stock; process for a few seconds. Strain through a fine sieve and add liquid to remaining stock. Combine prawn and chicken stocks. Season to taste with salt. Soak noodles in hot water for 10 minutes, drain in a colander.

Slice pork thinly. Wash and drain bean sprouts. Heat remaining peanut oil in a heavy saucepan and fry garlic and ginger gently. When they are golden add prawns and stir-fry 1 minute. Add stock, bring to boil, add noodles and cook for 3 minutes. Add pork and bean sprouts; heat through. Serve in a large bowl, garnished with sliced fish cakes, sprinkled with sesame oil, spring onion and cucumber.

One of the most popular quick meals cooked while you watch at street stalls. If you prepare the garnishes for this dish ahead, it is only a simple matter to assemble the ingredients. Serve with a bowl of Rojak (see p. 39).

FRIED NOODLES
Serves 4

- 500 g (1 lb) fresh yellow wheat noodles (Hokkien mee) or 250 g (8 oz) dried egg noodles
- 250 g (8 oz) cooked pork
- 250 g (8 oz) small cooked prawns
- 1 tablespoon canned salted black beans
- ¼ cup oil
- 2 teaspoons crushed garlic
- 2 teaspoons finely grated ginger
- 2 stalks celery, finely chopped
- 2 cups shredded white Chinese cabbage
- salt to taste

GARNISH
- 2-egg omelette, cut in strips
- oil for cooking
- 3 spring onions, sliced
- 2 fresh red chillies, sliced
- 2 teaspoons fried garlic (see Note)
- ¼ cup chopped fresh coriander

33

Rinse fresh noodles in hot water or cook dry noodles in boiling water. Drain. Slice pork finely and cut into narrow strips. Shell and devein prawns: if they are large, cut into pieces. Rinse black beans and mash with a fork.

When ready to serve heat a wok, add oil and when heated, stir-fry garlic over low heat, until it starts to change colour. Add ginger and black beans and stir-fry for 30 seconds.

Turn heat to high, add pork and fry, tossing, for 1 minute. Add prawns and stir for 1 minute. Add celery and Chinese cabbage and toss for 1 minute more. Add noodles and keep tossing until all ingredients are thoroughly mixed and noodles heated through. Add salt to taste.

Transfer to a large serving platter and sprinkle with prepared Garnish. Serve immediately.

Note   Ready fried garlic is sold in many Asian shops and saves time and effort. If you cannot find it, it is not difficult to make, especially if you start with dried garlic, either granulated or in slices. Granulated garlic is in most herb and spice ranges at supermarkets.

Put about 2 teaspoons into a fine metal tea strainer or other wire mesh strainer. Heat ½ cup oil in a wok until moderately hot and lower strainer into oil. Shake gently and lift out immediately the garlic turns golden. Do not allow to brown or it will taste bitter. Drain on paper towels. It might be worthwhile frying more than you need for one dish and when garlic is cool, store in an airtight bottle. Fresh garlic can be used, but after chopping finely, rinse in cold water and squeeze dry with paper towels before frying on low heat until pale golden.

Which Asian food enthusiast has not fallen under the spell of Laksa Lemak—noodles, seafood, rich coconut milk and spices.

SPICY PRAWN SOUP
Serves 4 to 6

- 750 g (1½ lb) raw prawns
- 1 tablespoon oil
- salt to taste
- 375 g (12 oz) rice vermicelli
- 250 g (8 oz) fresh bean sprouts
- 4 small, seedless green cucumbers
- small bunch fresh laksa leaves (see Note)
- sambal ulek
- fresh limes

SOUP
- 6 large dried red chillies
- 2 teaspoons dried shrimp paste (blacan)
- 2 medium onions, roughly chopped
- 2 teaspoons chopped galangal in brine or galangal powder
- 2 stems lemon grass, finely sliced or thinly peeled rind of 1 lemon
- 4 tablespoons peanut oil
- 1 teaspoon ground turmeric
- 1 tablespoon ground coriander
- 2 cups canned coconut milk
- salt to taste

Shell and devein prawns. Wash shells and heads thoroughly and drain well, reserving for stock.

Heat oil in a large saucepan, add prawn shells and heads and fry, stirring, until they turn red. Add 2 litres water and simmer, covered, for about 30 minutes. Strain stock and season to taste with salt. Discard shells and heads.

Place rice vermicelli in a bowl and cover with very hot water. Leave to soak. Pinch straggly tails off bean sprouts, wash well and drain in a colander. Wash cucumbers and cut into matchstick strips. Shred laksa leaves finely.

Soup Remove stems from dry chillies and shake out seeds. Soak chillies in hot water for 10 minutes. Drain and reserve a little of soaking water. Place chillies, with shrimp paste, onions, galangal and lemon grass or rind into a blender. Grind to a purée, adding a little chilli soaking water.

Heat 3 tablespoons of oil in a heavy saucepan and fry purée, stirring constantly, until fragrant and browned. Add turmeric and coriander and stir for 1 minute more. Add strained stock and simmer for 10 minutes. Before serving add coconut milk and drained rice vermicelli and bring to a simmer, adding more salt to taste if required. Heat remaining tablespoon of oil and stir-fry prawns just until they change colour—about 2 minutes. Season with salt to taste.

Serve soup in large bowls, topping each serve with bean sprouts, cucumber strips, a few prawns and shreds of laksa leaf. Offer sambal ulek and fresh lime wedges in small bowls as accompaniments to add extra piquancy to the meal.

Note Laksa leaves are sold in many countries as Vietnamese mint. It has a pointed leaf with a distinctive marking and a zingy, tongue-tingling taste.

Accompany this dish with rice or noodles.

DEEP-FRIED FISH WITH VEGETABLES
Serves 4

- 750 g (1½ lb) white fish fillets
- 1 teaspoon salt
- 2 teaspoons five spice powder
- 3 tablespoons cornflour
- 1 egg white, slightly beaten
- oil for frying
- extra teaspoon cornflour
- 1 clove garlic, crushed
- ½ teaspoon finely grated fresh ginger
- 2 cups sliced white Chinese cabbage
- 6 spring onions, sliced in 5 cm (2 inch) lengths
- 1 tablespoon light soy sauce
- 1 tablespoon oyster sauce

Cut fish fillets into finger-size pieces, discarding any bones. Mix salt, five spice powder and cornflour in a large bag. Pour egg white over fish and mix. Drop fish pieces into bag and shake well to coat. Dust off excess cornflour.

Heat oil in a wok and fry fish on high heat—about one quarter at a time—just until cooked through. This should take 1 to 2 minutes. Remove with slotted spoon as it cooks and drain on paper towel; keep warm. Mix teaspoon of cornflour with 1 tablespoon of cold water; set aside.

Pour off all but 1 tablespoon of oil from wok. Add garlic, ginger and cabbage; stir-fry for 1 minute. Add spring onions and stir-fry 1 minute more. Push to side of wok. Add soy and oyster sauces with ½ cup water; bring liquid to boil and add cornflour mixture. Stir until sauce boils and thickens. Pour into a dish, arrange fish pieces on top and serve immediately.

CHICKEN IN TAMARIND SAUCE
Serves 6

- *1.5 kg (3 lb) chicken pieces*
- *½ cup dried tamarind*
- *3 brown onions (or 20 small red onions), chopped*
- *3 tablespoons ground coriander*
- *3 tablespoons malt vinegar*
- *2 tablespoons dark soy sauce*
- *4 tablespoons sugar*
- *2 teaspoons ground black pepper*
- *2 teaspoons salt or to taste*
- *peanut oil for frying*
- *2 green cucumbers, thinly sliced*

Put chicken into a glass or earthenware bowl. Soak tamarind in 2 cups hot water for 10 minutes, squeeze firmly to dissolve pulp, strain through a nylon sieve and discard seeds. Grind onions to a purée with a food processor or blender. Add other ingredients except oil and cucumbers. Pour over chicken and put a weighted plate on top. Marinate for 8 hours. Cook in a stainless steel or enamel pan until chicken is tender. In a wok or frying pan heat a little oil and fry chicken pieces until browned. Arrange on plate and keep warm. Cook sauce on high heat until thick, stirring. Pour over chicken and serve with rice and cucumber.

A traditional salad eaten as a light meal or served as an accompaniment.

ROJAK
Serves 8

- *1 or 2 seedless cucumbers*
- *1 small pineapple, not too ripe*
- *1 yam bean or nashi fruit*
- *3 fresh red chillies*
- *8 squares fried bean curd*
- *salt*
- *1 teaspoon dried shrimp paste or to taste*
- *3 tablespoons white wine vinegar or lime juice*
- *2 tablespoons palm sugar or brown sugar*
- *2 teaspoons sambal ulek*

Wash cucumbers, mark skins with a fork and cut into slices. With a sharp knife peel and core pineapple and remove 'eyes' with a series of diagonal cuts. Slice flesh. Peel yam bean and slice. Seed and slice chillies. Halve bean curd diagonally and slice. Toss all with a little salt. Wrap shrimp paste in foil and grill about 5 minutes. Mix with remaining ingredients, pour over fruit and bean curd and toss well.

Malaysia

The preparation of this dish can be done a day ahead. It is then simply heated in the oven before serving. Garnish with cucumber and tomato slices or serve with a salad.

Spiced Seafood and Rice
Serves 6

- 1 kg (2 lb) firm white fish fillets
- lemon juice
- salt, pepper and ground turmeric
- 500 g (1 lb) raw prawns
- oil for frying
- 3 onions, finely chopped
- 3 cloves garlic, crushed
- 2 teaspoons finely grated fresh ginger
- 1 tablespoon ground coriander
- 2 teaspoons ground cummin
- 1 large ripe tomato, peeled and chopped
- salt to taste
- ¼ cup canned coconut milk

Spiced Rice
- 2 tablespoons ghee or oil
- 1 onion, finely sliced
- 1 quantity Whole Spice Mix (see p. iv)
- 500 g (1 lb) long grain rice
- 2 teaspoons salt or to taste

Wash fish fillets and cut each into 2 or 3 pieces, removing any bones. Sprinkle lightly with lemon juice and salt, pepper and ground turmeric. Set aside for 15 minutes. Meanwhile shell and devein prawns. Dry fish on paper towels and fry in about 1.5 cm (½ inch) of hot oil over medium heat, turning carefully to lightly brown both sides. Remove fish pieces as they are done.

Pour off excess oil, leaving about 2 tablespoons in pan. Fry onions, garlic and ginger, stirring frequently, until onion is soft and transparent. Add coriander, cummin and ½ teaspoon of turmeric. Stir for 1 minute longer. Stir in tomato, ½ cup water and salt to taste. Cover and simmer until tomato is soft and pulpy. Add coconut milk and simmer, uncovered, until mixture is smooth and very thick. Add fish and prawns, spooning sauce over, and simmer for a further few minutes. Turn off heat and leave while preparing Spiced Rice.

SPICED RICE   Heat all but a teaspoonful of ghee or oil and fry sliced onion until golden. Add Whole Spice Mix and rice and fry, stirring constantly, until rice is coated with ghee. Add 4 cups hot water and bring to boil. Stir in salt to taste, turn heat very low, cover and cook for 15 minutes. Remove from heat and set aside, covered, for 5 minutes. Remove whole spices.

Preheat oven to 160°C (325°F). Grease a baking dish with remaining teaspoon of ghee and spread one-third of Spiced Rice in one layer. On this spread a layer of fish mixture, another layer of Rice, then remaining fish mixture and a top layer of Rice. Cover and cook in oven for 25 minutes. Serve hot.

Vegetable Pickle

- *1 cup carrot sticks*
- *1 medium yam bean, peeled*
- *1 cup young green beans, trimmed*
- *10 fresh red chillies*
- *12 small whole shallots or onions*
- *3 small seedless cucumbers*
- *2 tablespoons peanut oil*
- *2 cloves garlic, finely grated*
- *2 teaspoons finely grated fresh ginger*
- *1 teaspoon ground turmeric*
- *½ cup white vinegar*
- *2 teaspoons sugar*
- *1 teaspoon salt*
- *toasted crushed peanuts*

Cut carrots and yam bean into strips. Cut beans into pieces of same length. Discard stems from chillies, leaving them whole. Wash cucumbers, cut in chunks.

Heat oil in a saucepan and fry garlic and ginger over low heat for 1 minute. Add turmeric and fry for a few seconds longer. Add vinegar, sugar and salt and ½ cup water. Bring to boil and add all vegetables except cucumbers. Return to boil and cook for 3 minutes. Add cucumber and boil for 1 minute more. Turn into a bowl and leave to cool. The pickle can be used immediately or transferred to a jar and stored for up to 2 weeks in the refrigerator. Sprinkle with toasted crushed peanuts to serve.

Fresh rice noodles are now available in most Asian grocery stores and make the basis of a quick, tasty meal.

FRIED RICE NOODLES
Serves 6 to 8

- 1 kg (2 lb) fresh rice noodles (see Note)
- 125 g (4 oz) roasted or barbecued pork
- 250 g (8 oz) small raw prawns
- 250 g (8 oz) small cleaned squid
- 2 Chinese sausages (lap cheong)
- 1 cup fresh bean sprouts
- 4 tablespoons oil
- 6 cloves garlic, finely chopped
- 4 small onions, sliced
- 4 fresh red chillies, seeded and chopped
- 2 tablespoons dark soy sauce
- 2 tablespoons oyster sauce
- 3 eggs, beaten
- 1 cup chopped spring onions, including green

Cut noodles into strips about the size of fettucine. Cut pork into thin slices. Shell and devein prawns. Slice squid thinly. Steam Chinese sausages for 10 minutes and cut into very thin diagonal slices. Wash bean sprouts and pinch off any straggly ends. Drain.

Heat 2 tablespoons of oil in a wok and fry garlic, onions

and chillies over medium heat, stirring, until soft. Add pork, prawns, squid and sausage slices and stir-fry for 2 to 3 minutes, or until seafood is cooked. Add bean sprouts and toss once or twice, then remove mixture from wok and set aside. Heat remaining oil in wok, and when very hot toss noodles until heated through. Add soy and oyster sauces and toss well. Remove from wok. Pour in beaten egg and stir constantly until set. Return reserved fried mixture to wok, and toss well. Serve hot, garnished with spring onions.

Note Known in Malaysia as 'kway teow', fresh rice noodles can also be purchased in Chinese food stores as 'sa hor fun'. Best used on day of purchase as refrigerating makes them hard.

In Malaysia this dish would be cooked with goat's meat but you can substitute it with mutton or lamb. Serve with Vegetable Pickle (see p. 42) and Roti (see p. 46).

Spicy Mutton Curry and Roti
Serves 6

- *1 kg (2 lb) mutton or lamb*
- *4 tablespoons desiccated coconut*
- *1 walnut-size piece of tamarind pulp*
- *2 large onions, roughly chopped*
- *4 cloves garlic*
- *1 tablespoon roughly chopped fresh ginger*
- *2 tablespoons Ground Spices II (see p. iv)*
- *6 dried red chillies*
- *1 stalk lemon grass, finely sliced,
  or 1 teaspoon finely chopped lemon rind*
- *2 tablespoons peanut oil*
- *2 ripe tomatoes, chopped*
- *¾ cup canned coconut milk*
- *salt to taste*

Cut meat into small cubes. Toast coconut in a dry frying pan, stirring constantly over medium low heat, until it is a rich golden brown. Set aside. Put tamarind pulp in a small bowl and cover with ½ cup very hot water. Leave for 5 minutes, then knead to dissolve. Strain through a fine sieve. Put tamarind liquid in blender container with onions, garlic, ginger, spices, dried chillies, lemon grass or rind and toasted coconut. Blend until smooth.

Heat oil in a large saucepan and fry blended mixture for 5 minutes, stirring frequently as it starts to cook, then constantly towards the end so that it does not stick and burn. Add meat and fry, stirring well. Add tomatoes and stir. Add coconut milk mixed with an equal amount of water, and 1 teaspoon salt. Bring slowly to simmering point and simmer, uncovered, until meat is tender, stirring occasionally.

ROTI (FLAT BREAD)
Makes about 12

- *4 cups plain flour*
- *2 teaspoons baking powder*
- *1 cup desiccated coconut*
- *2 teaspoons salt*
- *2 teaspoons butter*
- *1 tablespoon finely chopped onion*
- *2 teaspoons finely chopped, fresh red chilli*
- *1 egg, beaten*
- *oil for cooking*

In a large bowl mix flour, baking powder, coconut and salt. Rub in butter until evenly distributed. Stir onion and chilli through flour, then add egg and about 2 cups water to bind mixture to a stiff dough. Knead until it forms into a ball and is no longer sticky. Set aside to rest for 30 minutes.

Take pieces of dough about the the size of a lemon and pat between floured hands or roll on a floured board to make circles the size of large saucers. Cook on a lightly greased hot griddle or heavy frying pan until golden. Serve hot.

Burma

Moh hin gha—the national dish of Burma. A one-course meal you will find being sold everywhere—in markets, at roadside stalls and by itinerant vendors. An essential ingredient of this curried fish soup is the tender heart of a banana tree. Because few people have easy access to banana trees, canned bamboo shoots can be used, although the result is not as good. If you do wish to make the authentic dish, however, see Note 2 for preparing the banana heart. Serve accompaniments in separate bowls and add according to individual preference.

Fish Soup with Rice Vermicelli
Serves 6 to 8

- 4 medium onions, roughly chopped
- 6 cloves garlic, peeled
- 2 teaspoons chopped fresh ginger
- 1 teaspoon ground turmeric
- 2 fresh chillies, seeded and chopped,
  or ½ teaspoon chilli powder, optional
- 2 tablespoons sesame oil
- 4 tablespoons peanut oil
- 2 cans of herrings in tomato sauce (see Note 1)
- 3½ cups canned coconut milk
- small can bamboo shoots, drained and sliced,
  or banana heart (see Note 2)
- 1 teaspoon dried shrimp paste
- 3 tablespoons fish sauce

- 3 tablespoons chick pea flour
- 2 tablespoons lemon juice
- 500 g (1 lb) fine egg noodles or rice vermicelli

ACCOMPANIMENTS
- finely sliced spring onions, including green portion
- chopped fresh coriander leaves
- finely sliced white onion
- roasted chick peas, finely ground in a blender or crushed with mortar and pestle
- crisp fried noodles, broken into small pieces
- Fried Onion Flakes (see p. 22)
- thin slices of garlic, fried in oil until golden
- wedges of lemon
- dried chillies, fried in oil for a few seconds
- chilli powder

Put onions, garlic, ginger, turmeric and chilli powder in a blender and blend to a purée. Heat both oils in a large saucepan and when hot add blended ingredients and chillies (be careful as the hot oil will sputter). Reduce heat and stir well so that ingredients are mixed with oil. Cover pan and simmer mixture, stirring frequently with a wooden spoon. This method of cooking will produce a mellow flavour and frying should take at least 15 minutes. If mixture starts to stick to pan before onions are soft and transparent, add a tablespoon of water from time to time and stir well. Mixture is ready when water content of onions has reduced and ingredients are a rich red-brown colour, with oil appearing around edge of mass.

Add liquid from cans of herrings, 1½ cups of canned coconut milk, 2½ cups water and sliced bamboo shoots. Bring to boil, then turn heat low and simmer for 15 minutes. (If using banana heart slices, simmer until tender.) Dissolve dried shrimp paste in fish sauce and add to mixture. Mix chick pea flour with a cup of cold water until smooth and add to pan. Stir constantly as it comes to boil. Simmer for 5 minutes, then add herrings, remaining 2 cups of coconut milk and lemon juice. Stir mixture as it comes to simmering point.

Cook noodles in boiling salted water, just until tender. Drain well and serve in a large bowl alongside soup. Set out small bowls with accompaniments on table. Transfer fish soup to a tureen or other large receptacle and provide deep bowls

or old-fashioned soup plates. Put noodles into bowl first, then ladle piping hot soup over top. Accompaniments are added by each person as desired.

Note 1   In Burma a strong-flavoured, bony fish is used for this dish, but since most people have a horror of fish bones you can also use the equally tasty canned fish in which the bones are softened down.

Note 2   If you have a banana tree which can be used for this dish you must protect your hands with gloves and clothing with an old apron. Be warned: the sap from the banana tree leaves a stain that is impossible to remove! Use about 30 cm (12 inches) of the tender heart of the tree. Peel off outer layers and discard. Cut inner portion across into thin slices. Soak in a large basin of salted water for several hours. The sticky juice will form hair-like strands. Pull these away and discard.

This Burmese curry is served with plain or Coconut Rice (see p. 51) and accompaniments such as Dry Prawn Relish (see p. 52) and Cucumber Pickle (see p. 53).

CHICKEN CURRY WITH PUMPKIN
Serves 4 to 6

- *1 x 1.5 kg (3 lb) chicken*
- *3 medium onions, roughly chopped*
- *6 cloves garlic*
- *2 teaspoons grated fresh ginger*
- *1 stalk lemon grass, thinly sliced or 2 strips lemon rind*
- *2 tablespoons vegetable oil*
- *1 tablespoon sesame oil*
- *2 teaspoons salt or to taste*
- *1 teaspoon turmeric*
- *1 teaspoon chilli powder, optional*
- *1 cup chopped or canned tomatoes*
- *2 cups cubed pumpkin*
- *1 tablespoon fish sauce*
- *2 tablespoons lemon juice*
- *1 tablespoon chopped fresh coriander leaves*
- *¼ teaspoon ground cardamom*

Cut chicken into serving pieces (or purchase chicken joints). Put onions, garlic, ginger, lemon grass or rind into a blender. Blend to a smooth purée, adding a little oil. Heat remaining oil in a saucepan and when very hot add blended mixture, salt, turmeric and chilli powder. Fry over medium heat, stirring constantly with a wooden spoon. If mixture starts to stick to base of pan, add a little water. Simmer over low heat until mixture turns a rich red-brown.

At this point ingredients will begin to stick to pan: keep stirring while adding chicken pieces. Turn pieces in mixture until thoroughly coated. Cover and simmer until half-cooked— about 20 minutes.

Add 1 cup water, tomato, pumpkin, fish sauce and lemon juice. Continue cooking until chicken and pumpkin are tender, stirring occasionally. Finally stir in coriander leaves and cardamom. Serve with rice.

COCONUT RICE
Serves 6

- *500 g (1 lb) long grain rice*
- *1 x 400 mL (14 fl oz) can coconut milk*
- *2 teaspoons salt*

Put rice, coconut milk, 600 mL (1 pint) water and salt into a saucepan and bring to boil. Turn heat very low, stir well, then cover tightly and cook for 20 minutes without lifting lid. If all liquid is not absorbed at the end of this time, stir very lightly around edges of pan with a fork, just to mix in coconut milk. Replace lid and continue cooking over very low heat for a further 5 to 10 minutes. Serve hot.

This is a popular acccompaniment: you can keep it stored in an airtight jar for weeks, in the refrigerator for months . . . if you hide it well!

Dry Prawn Relish

- ½ cup dried garlic slices or 10 cloves garlic
- 1 cup dried onion slices or 4 medium onions
- 2 cups peanut oil
- 1 x 250 g (8 oz) packet prawn powder
- 2 teaspoons chilli powder
- 2 teaspoons salt
- 1 teaspoon dried shrimp paste
- ½ cup vinegar

If you can purchase fried garlic slices and fried shallots from Asian stores it will save you a lot of trouble, but if not peel garlic cloves and cut into thin slices of even thickness. Slice onions finely. Heat oil and fry onion and garlic separately over low heat until golden. Lift out with frying spatula and set aside on paper towel. They will become crisp and darken as they cool. (If using dried onion and garlic, be careful not to have the oil too hot as they cook very quickly and burn easily. Cook only until they start to colour a pale gold.)

Pour off oil and reserve, leaving about 1 cup in pan. Add prawn powder and fry over low heat for 5 minutes. All prawn powder should be moistened by oil. If oil is insufficient, add a little more from reserved oil. Add chilli powder, salt and shrimp paste mixed with vinegar. Stir well and fry until crisp. Cool completely, then stir in fried onion and garlic until well mixed.

CUCUMBER PICKLE
Serves 6

- 2 large green cucumbers
- ½ cup cider vinegar
- 1 teaspoon salt
- 2 tablespoons sesame seeds
- 2 tablespoons peanut oil
- 2 tablespoons sesame oil
- 2 tablespoons fried onions (see Note)
- 2 tablespoons fried garlic

Peel cucumbers and cut in halves lengthwise. Scoop out seeds with a teaspoon. Cut cucumber into pencil strips, then cut these strips across into 5 cm (2 inch) pieces. Mix vinegar and salt with 2 cups water in a saucepan. Bring to boil; drop in cucumbers and boil 2 to 3 minutes—do not overcook. Drain immediately and leave to cool.

Toast sesame seeds in a dry frying pan, stirring constantly, until evenly browned. Turn onto a plate to cool. Mix peanut and sesame oil and drizzle over cucumbers, mixing well with fingers. Add fried onion, garlic and sesame seeds; toss lightly. Transfer to a small serving dish.

Note If unable to buy ready-fried sliced onions and garlic, heat both oils together and fry finely sliced garlic until pale golden. Drain on paper towel. Fry finely sliced onion until golden brown. Remove from oil and drain. Cool oil before dressing cucumbers.

THAILAND

For Thai meals, the best kind of rice to use is the slightly fragrant, long grain white rice known as jasmine rice. It is a variety, not a brand name.

STEAMED RICE
Serves 6 to 8

- *500g (1 lb) jasmine rice*
- *3 cups water*

If rice needs washing, wash well, then drain thoroughly in a sieve. Place in a saucepan with water and bring to boil. Lower heat to medium and cook, uncovered, until water is absorbed and holes appear on surface of rice mass. Remove from heat, scoop rice into a steamer or colander and steam over fast-boiling water for 25 to 30 minutes. The grains will be firm and separate.

A quicker method is to cook rice in a saucepan, but once water comes to boil keep lid firmly on pot and make sure heat is turned as low as possible. It should be ready in 15 minutes.

This soup has a wide variety of textures and flavours and is perfect for a light meal.

COMBINATION SOUP
Serves 4

- 6 dried shiitake (Chinese) mushrooms
- 250 g (8 oz) boneless pork
- 250 g (8 oz) chicken thigh fillet
- 250 g (8 oz) shelled raw prawns
- 100 g (3½ oz) bean thread vermicelli
- 2 tablespoons oil
- 2 teaspoons Pepper and Coriander Paste (see p. 56)
- 8 cups pork or chicken stock
- 1 tablespoon Maggi Seasoning (see Note)
- 1 tablespoon fish sauce
- 2 small seedless green cucumbers
- 6 spring onions, sliced
- sliced red chilli
- chopped fresh coriander leaves
- sliced spring onion tops

Soak dried mushrooms in hot water for 30 minutes. Squeeze out excess moisture. Discard stems and slice caps. Slice pork into thin strips. Cut chicken into slices. Devein prawns; cut into halves if large. Soak bean thread vermicelli in hot water for 10 to 15 minutes, then drain.

Heat oil and fry Pepper and Coriander Paste, stirring, until fragrant. Add pork and chicken and stir-fry until colour changes. Add stock, seasoning, fish sauce, sliced mushrooms and noodles. Bring to boil and simmer for 15 minutes.

Wash cucumbers and slice into small chunks. Stir into soup with spring onions and prawns and cook for 3 to 4 minutes. Serve immediately sprinkled with sliced chilli, chopped coriander and spring onion tops.

Note Maggi Seasoning, a Swiss-made sauce found in most supermarkets, is a good substitute for Thai Golden Mountain Sauce.

Fresh coriander is essential to Thai cooking and this paste is a useful one to have on hand—just store it in a jar in the refrigerator.

PEPPER AND CORIANDER PASTE
Makes about 1 cup

- *1 tablespoon chopped garlic*
- *2 teaspoons salt*
- *1 tablespoon whole black peppercorns*
- *2 cups coarsely chopped fresh coriander, including roots*
- *4 tablespoons lemon juice*

Crush garlic with salt to a smooth paste. Roast peppercorns in a dry pan for a minute or two. Finely chop coriander roots, leaves and stems. Mix all ingredients with lemon juice and grind in blender, adding a little water if necessary.

Once the preparation is done, this is a fast-cooking combination dish ideal for a one-course meal.

MIXED FRIED VERMICELLI
Serves 4

- 250 g (8 oz) rice vermicelli
- 10 dried shiitake (Chinese) mushrooms
- 250 g (8 oz) pork fillet
- 375 g (12 oz) small raw prawns
- 8 spring onions
- 1 canned bamboo shoot
- 2 young carrots
- 2 tablespoons peanut oil
- 3 teaspoons Pepper and Coriander Paste (see p. 56)
- 3 tablespoons fish sauce
- 1 tablespoon white wine vinegar
- 2 teaspoons sugar
- 2 tablespoons Fried Onion Flakes (see p. 22)
- 3 tablespoons chopped fresh coriander leaves
- 2 fresh red chillies, seeded and sliced diagonally

Soak vermicelli in hot water for 10 minutes, then drain. Soak mushrooms in hot water for 30 minutes, squeeze out water, discard stems and slice caps thinly. Cut pork into thin shreds. Shell and devein prawns. Finely slice spring onions. Cut bamboo shoot and carrots into julienne strips.

Heat oil in a wok and fry Pepper and Coriander Paste on low heat, stirring, until fragrant. Add pork and mushrooms. Stir-fry on medium heat, tossing, until cooked. Add prawns, spring onions, bamboo shoot and carrots and stir-fry for a further 3 minutes. Stir in fish sauce, vinegar and sugar. Add vermicelli and toss until heated through. Garnish with Fried Onion Flakes, coriander leaves and chillies.

RED CURRY PASTE

Makes 1 cup

- *8 large dried red chillies*
- *2 small brown onions, chopped*
- *1 teaspoon black peppercorns*
- *2 teaspoons ground cummin*
- *1 tablespoon ground coriander*
- *2 tablespoons chopped fresh coriander roots*
- *1 teaspoon salt*
- *1 stem lemon grass, finely sliced or 2 strips lemon rind*
- *2 teaspoons chopped galangal in brine*
- *1 tablespoon chopped garlic*
- *2 teaspoons dried shrimp paste*
- *1 tablespoon oil*
- *1 teaspoon turmeric*
- *2 teaspoons paprika*

Remove stems from chillies. (If you want curry to be as hot as it is in Thailand, leave seeds in.) Break chillies into pieces and soak in just enough water to cover for 10 minutes, then place in an electric blender with other ingredients. Blend to a smooth paste, stopping frequently to push ingredients down with a spatula. You may need to add an extra tablespoon of water to assist blending.

All that is needed to accompany this dish is a bowl of rice.

CHICKEN AND VEGETABLES WITH SHRIMP SAUCE
Serves 4

- 4 large chicken thigh pieces
- 3 cups mixed vegetables
- ½ cup dried shrimp
- 3 fresh red chillies
- 3 cloves garlic
- 1 cup canned coconut milk
- 2 tablespoons palm sugar or brown sugar
- 2 tablespoons fish sauce
- 1 tablespoon lime or lemon juice
- 1 tablespoon tamarind pulp

TOPPING
- ½ cup canned coconut milk
- ½ teaspoon salt
- 1 teaspoon rice flour
- ¼ cup crushed toasted peanuts

Steam or poach chicken until cooked. Leave to cool, then discard skin and bones; cut meat into thick slices. Blanch each vegetable separately in lightly salted, boiling water until tender but still crisp. Refresh in iced water to stop cooking and set colour. Drain.

Soak dried shrimp in hot water for 10 minutes. Chop chillies and pound to a paste with shrimp and garlic. Heat ½ cup of coconut milk until oily, add chilli mixture and fry, stirring, for a few minutes. Stir in palm sugar, fish sauce, lime juice and tamarind. Gradually stir in remaining coconut milk and simmer until reduced. The sauce will darken.

Arrange vegetables on a serving plate. Place sliced chicken on top and pour sauce over. Add Topping and serve.

TOPPING Heat coconut milk, salt and rice flour in a small pan, stirring until it thickens. Spoon over chicken and sprinkle with toasted peanuts.

Serve with steamed jasmine rice.

BEEF AND SPINACH IN COCONUT MILK
Serves 4–6

- *500 g (1 lb) spinach*
- *500 g (1 lb) lean round steak*
- *1 x 400 mL can coconut milk*
- *3 tablespoons Pepper and Coriander Paste (see p. 56)*
- *2 stalks tender lemon grass, finely sliced*
- *1 tablespoon sliced bottled galangal*
- *2 tablespoons fish sauce*
- *1 tablespoon palm sugar or brown sugar*

Wash spinach well, trim and discard stems. Cut leaves across twice. Slice beef into paper-thin strips. Put coconut milk in a wok or large pan; add 2 cups water, Pepper and Coriander Paste, lemon grass, galangal, fish sauce and sugar. Stir over medium heat until mixture reaches simmering point. Add beef and cook gently, uncovered, for 20 minutes or until beef is almost tender. Add spinach and cook until wilted.

Serve this dish with steamed rice.

STEAMED FISH PUDDING
Serves 4

- 750 g (1½ lb) *fish fillets*
- 1½ tablespoons Red Curry Paste (see p. 58)
- 1 teaspoon chopped lesser galangal
- ½ teaspoon finely grated lime rind
- 2 tablespoons fish sauce
- 1 egg, beaten
- 1 cup canned coconut milk
- 2 teaspoons rice flour
- 3 tablespoons finely chopped spring onions, green parts included
- 2 tablespoons fresh coriander leaves
- about 20 small basil leaves

Remove any skin and bones from fish and cut into thin slices. Mix Red Curry Paste and fish sauce to a smooth paste.

Transfer paste to a large bowl. Add sliced fish, egg and half the coconut milk. Mix well until liquid has been absorbed into fish. Oil a heatproof dish and turn fish mixture into this. Mix rice flour with remaining coconut milk, add good pinch of salt and pour over fish. Sprinkle with spring onions. Set the dish on a trivet in a pan of boiling water, cover and steam until firm and opaque, about 25 minutes. Leave to cool slightly and firm up before serving. Garnish with coriander and basil leaves.

CHILLI FRIED RICE
Serves 4

- *3 tablespoons peanut oil*
- *1 large onion, finely chopped*
- *1 fresh red chilli, seeded and sliced*
- *1 fresh green chilli, seeded and sliced*
- *1 tablespoon Red Curry Paste (see p. 58)*
- *250g (8 oz) boneless pork, finely diced*
- *500 g (1 lb) raw prawns, shelled and deveined*
- *flesh from 1 cooked crab or 185 g (6 oz) crab meat*
- *4 cups cold steamed rice*
- *3 eggs, beaten*
- *salt and pepper to taste*
- *2 tablespoons fish sauce*
- *1 cup chopped spring onions, including green tops*
- *½ cup chopped fresh coriander leaves*

Heat oil in a wok and fry onion and sliced chillies until soft, stirring frequently. Add Red Curry Paste and fry until oil separates from mixture. Add pork and stir-fry until cooked, then add prawns (chopped into pieces if they are very large). Cook, stirring, until prawns start to turn pink, then add crab. Add rice and toss thoroughly until coated with curry mixture and heated through.

Push rice mixture to one side of wok and pour beaten eggs, seasoned with salt and pepper, into centre of wok. Stir until eggs are almost set, then increase heat to high and mix eggs through rice. Sprinkle fish sauce evenly over rice and mix well. Remove from heat and stir spring onions through. Serve garnished with coriander leaves.

CAMBODIA, LAOS AND VIETNAM

BEEF WITH SESAME SAUCE
Serves 4

- *500 g (1 lb) rump or fillet steak*
  - *1 tablespoon soy sauce*
  - *3 tablespoons peanut oil*
  - *1 clove garlic, crushed*
- *1 cup tender green beans, trimmed and sliced*
  - *½ cup sliced bamboo shoots*
  - *½ cup beef stock*
  - *3 teaspoons cornflour*
- *1 cup sliced stalks from Chinese cabbage*
- *2 teaspoons sesame paste or smooth peanut butter*
- *1 tablespoon Garlic, Chilli and Lime Sauce (see p. 66)*

Slice beef paper thin. Sprinkle with soy and mix well. Heat oil in a wok, add garlic and meat and stir-fry over high heat until meat changes colour. Add beans and bamboo shoots and fry for 1 minute. Add stock mixed with cornflour, stirring until it thickens. Add Chinese cabbage and cook 1 minute. Stir in sesame paste and Sauce. Serve immediately.

Note Sesame paste is very stiff and difficult to spoon out of the bottle or can. Smooth peanut butter gives very much the same flavour, so if you feel unwilling to search for and tussle with sesame paste, the answer is probably in your pantry!

The title of this dish comes from bean starch noodles known as 'long rice'. Serve it with Garlic, Chilli and Lime Sauce (see p. 66).

LONG RICE WITH CHICKEN AND YAM BEAN
Serves 4

- *500 g (1 lb) chicken thigh fillets*
- *2 teaspoons crushed garlic*
- *250 g (8 oz) bean thread vermicelli*
- *2 tablespoons peanut oil*
- *1 medium onion, cut into wedges and layers separated*
- *2 small yam beans or large white radish, cut into strips*
- *2 tablespoons fish sauce*
- *¼ teaspoon black pepper*
- *½ cup chicken stock or water*

Cut chicken meat into bite-size pieces. Mix with crushed garlic. Soak vermicelli in hot water for 15 minutes, then drop into lightly salted, boiling water and cook for 10 minutes or until tender. Drain.

Heat peanut oil in a wok and stir-fry chicken, tossing over high heat until colour changes. Push to side of wok. Add onion pieces and vegetable strips and fry for 1 minute, then draw chicken into centre of wok and add fish sauce, pepper and stock. Cook for 2 minutes longer. Add drained noodles and stir until thoroughly combined. Serve immediately.

*An unusual combination, this Vietnamese recipe makes a complete
meal in a bowl.*

BEEF SOUP WITH SALAD
Serves 6

- 2 kg (4 lb) beef brisket on the bone
- 500 g (1 lb) shin beef
- 2 onions, sliced
- 5 cm (2 inch) piece fresh ginger, sliced
- stick of cinnamon
- 5 whole star anise
- 1 teaspoon whole black peppercorns
- salt to taste
- 375 g (12 oz) packet dried rice sticks (Banh Pho)
- 250 g (½ lb) fresh bean sprouts
- 4 spring onions
- 3 firm ripe tomatoes
- 2 white onions
- 500 g (1 lb) rump or fillet steak
- fish sauce
- lemon wedges
- fresh red chillies, chopped
- chopped fresh coriander leaves
- fresh mint leaves

Put beef in a large saucepan. Add cold water to cover with

onions, ginger, cinnamon, star anise and peppercorns. Bring to boil, turn heat very low, cover and simmer for 6 hours. The success of this dish depends on a really strong stock. Add salt to taste. Strain, chill and remove fat.

Soak rice sticks in hot water for 10 minutes or boil for 2 minutes. Drain.

Rinse bean sprouts with cold water and pinch off any straggly roots. Slice spring onions finely. Cut tomatoes in half lengthwise, then slice each half. Peel and thinly slice white onions. Slice steak into paper-thin, bite-size pieces (this is easier if you partially freeze the meat).

Put a serving of noodles and a handful of bean sprouts in each large soup bowl. Place a few slices of beef, tomato and onions in a large ladle; immerse ladle in boiling stock until beef is pink—do not overcook. Pour contents of ladle over noodles and bean sprouts. Fish sauce, a squeeze of lemon juice, chillies, coriander and mint leaves are added to individual bowls to taste.

GARLIC, CHILLI AND LIME SAUCE

- *2 ripe red chillies*
- *1 clove garlic, finely chopped*
- *1 tablespoon sugar*
- *1 lime*
- *1 tablespoon vinegar*
- *4 tablespoons fish sauce*

Cut off stalks from chillies, split down centre and with the point of a sharp knife remove seeds. Chop finely or pound in a mortar and pestle with garlic. Add sugar. Cut lime in half and squeeze on a citrus juicer. Add juice and pulp to chillies. Stir in vinegar, fish sauce and 2 tablespoons water. Serve in a small bowl and add sparingly!

STEAMED FISH WITH NOODLES
Serves 4 to 6

- *100 g (3½ oz) bean thread vermicelli*
- *6 dried shiitake (Chinese) mushrooms*
- *2 carrots*
- *3 thin slices fresh ginger*
- *1 large clove garlic*
- *2 tablespoons fish sauce*
- *750 g (1½ lb) firm white fish fillets*
- *½ cup canned coconut milk*
- *1 teaspoon rice flour*
- *fresh coriander leaves*
- *finely sliced spring onions*

Soak noodles and mushrooms in separate bowls of hot water to cover for 30 minutes. Simmer mushrooms 15 minutes and cool, discard stems and slice caps thinly. Drain noodles and cut in short lengths. Peel carrots and cut into matchstick strips. Cut ginger into thin shreds and finely chop garlic. Combine all these ingredients with fish sauce; place in a heatproof dish in a steamer, cover and steam for 15 minutes. Arrange fish fillets over noodle mixture. Steam until fish is opaque.

Heat coconut milk in a small pan with rice flour and ¼ teaspoon salt until thickened. Pour over fish and serve garnished with coriander leaves and spring onion.

THE PHILIPPINES

SOUR SOUP OF BEEF
Serves 6

- 500 g (1 lb) shin beef
- 1 kg (2 lb) soup bones
- 250 g (8 oz) lean boneless pork
- 1 medium onion, sliced
- 2 green tomatoes, sliced
- ½ cup bottled green tamarind
- salt to taste
- 1 large sweet potato, peeled and diced
- 1 giant white radish (daikon), sliced
- 2 cups shredded sorrel or spinach leaves
- fish sauce to taste
- lime or lemon wedges

Put beef, bones and pork into a large saucepan with water to cover. Add onion, tomatoes, tamarind and salt. Bring to boil, then reduce heat and simmer, covered, until meat is tender. Remove meat to cool.

Slice pork thinly and cut beef into dice. Discard bones. Add sweet potato and radish and simmer until almost soft. Add sorrel; season soup to taste with fish sauce. Return to boil and as soon as leaves are cooked return meat to soup. Serve with lime or lemon wedges to add extra piquancy.

Serve this stew with white rice and small bowls of extra fish sauce, soy sauce, a hot chilli sauce or a traditional Filipino mixture of equal quantities of bottled shrimp sauce and lime juice.

BEEF AND VEGETABLE STEW
Serves 6

- 1 oxtail, jointed
- 750 g (1½ lb) shin beef on bone, sliced
- 3 teaspoons salt, or to taste
- 3 tablespoons vegetable oil
- 2 teaspoons annatto seeds
- 2 large onions, sliced very finely
- 8 large cloves garlic, finely chopped
- 1 teaspoon ground black pepper
- 3 tablespoons roasted rice powder
- ½ cup roasted peanuts, crushed or pounded
- 250 g (8 oz) tender green beans, cut in halves
- 4 slender eggplants, halved lengthways
- 2 tablespoons fish sauce, or to taste
- 2 tablespoons sliced spring onion, including green parts
- 2 tablespoons chopped celery leaves

Put oxtail and shin of beef into a large pan with water to cover and salt to taste. Bring to boil and simmer until almost tender, about 2 hours. Cool to lukewarm and strain. Chill stock and remove fat from surface. (Use a pressure cooker if you have one: put oxtail and shin into cooker with just enough water to cover and salt to taste. Cook under pressure for 1 hour.)

Dry pieces of partially cooked meats with paper towel. Heat 1 tablespoon oil in a large, deep saucepan or flameproof casserole and brown pieces, a few at a time, turning with tongs. Transfer each batch to a plate as it cooks. Pour off any fat from pan and heat remaining oil; fry annatto seeds on low heat for 1 minute, covering pan as they pop when they become hot. Remove pan from heat and lift out seeds on a slotted spoon. The oil will now have become a bright orange colour. Add onions and garlic and fry over medium heat, stirring frequently, until soft—about 10 minutes. Return meat to pan. Reheat stock, adding sufficient hot water to make 8 cups. Pour over meat, add pepper and bring to boil. Turn heat low and simmer, partially covered, until meat is tender.

Meanwhile combine roasted rice powder (sold in Asian stores) with peanuts. If rice powder is not readily available, make it at home—the flavour is essential in this dish. Put rice into a heavy frying pan and roast over medium heat, stirring frequently, and shaking pan so that grains colour evenly. When deep golden, allow to cool slightly, then grind to a powder in an electric blender.

Test meat which should be tender enough to easily pierce with a fork, but not falling off bone. Add more water to just cover meat if necessary. Add rice and peanut mixture, stirring until smooth. Stir beans and eggplant into stew and cook, uncovered, until vegetables are tender. Add fish sauce to taste. Serve hot, sprinkled with spring onion and celery leaves.

This combination dish is one of many found in the Philippines with a Spanish origin . . . in this case, the famous paella.

RICE WITH CHICKEN AND SEAFOOD
Serves 6 to 8

- 1.5 kg (3 lb) chicken pieces
- salt and pepper to taste
- 500 g (1 lb) boneless pork
- 2 chorizo (hot Spanish) or other spicy sausages
- 750 g (1½ lb) raw prawns
- 500 g (1 lb) fresh mussels
- olive oil for frying

SOFRITO
- 4 tablespoons olive oil
- 3 large onions, finely chopped
- 1 teaspoon saffron strands
- 6 cloves garlic, finely chopped
- 2 large ripe tomatoes, peeled and chopped
- 3 teaspoons salt, or to taste
- 3 teaspoons paprika
- 500 g (1 lb) long grain rice
- 4½ cups hot chicken stock
- 1 cup frozen peas
- strips of bottled pimiento or red capsicum

71

Season pieces of chicken with salt and pepper. Cut pork into cubes, discarding any skin. Pierce skin of chorizos here and there; put into a saucepan with water to cover and bring to boil. Reduce heat and simmer for 5 minutes; drain and slice into rounds. Wash prawns, but do not shell. Scrub mussels under running water with a stiff brush; remove beards, discarding any mussels which don't have closed shells.

In a large, heavy frying pan or paella pan heat sufficient olive oil to cover the base and brown chicken pieces on all sides. Transfer to a plate. Brown chorizo slices and pork and drain on paper towel. Discard oil remaining in pan.

SOFRITO   Clean pan and add olive oil; fry onions over medium heat until soft and golden, stirring frequently. Heat saffron strands briefly in a dry pan—do not let them burn. Crush with the back of a spoon, and dissolve in 2 tablespoons boiling water. Add garlic, saffron and tomatoes to onions. Fry, stirring, until tomatoes are soft and pulpy. Add salt, paprika and rice, stir over medium heat for 3 to 4 minutes. Add hot stock and stir while bringing to boil.

Add chicken pieces, pork and sliced sausages. Cover and cook over very low heat for 15 minutes. Add prawns and mussels. Do not stir, but push mussels into mass of rice so that they cook in the steam. Scatter peas over top. Cover and cook for a further 15 minutes. Rice should be cooked through and all liquid absorbed. Decorate top with strips of pimiento or red capsicum. Serve immediately.

A one-pot meal which provides both a soup and a meat and vegetable dish. Accompany it with plain rice.

POCHERO
Serves 6

- 250 g (8 oz) dried chickpeas
- 500 g (1 lb) boneless pork
- 2 chorizo (hot Spanish) sausages
- 1.5 kg (3 lb) chicken pieces
- 1 large onion, sliced
- salt to taste
- 1 teaspoon whole black peppercorns
- 4 tablespoons oil
- 10 cloves garlic, finely chopped
- 1 medium onion, finely chopped
- 2 ripe tomatoes, peeled and diced
- 500 g (1 lb) sweet potatoes, peeled and cut into chunks
- ½ white Chinese cabbage cut across in 5 cm (2 inch) sections
- 8 spring onions, cut in 5 cm (2 inch) lengths

Wash chickpeas and soak overnight in plenty of water to cover. Cut pork into large cubes. Slice chorizos across into 2.5 cm (1 inch) pieces. Drain chickpeas and put into a large saucepan with pork, chorizo slices, chicken pieces and water to cover. Add sliced onion, salt and peppercorns and bring to boil. Reduce heat, cover and simmer until meat and chickpeas are almost tender.

In a separate pan heat oil and fry garlic and chopped onion over low heat, stirring frequently, until golden brown. Add tomatoes and cook to a pulp. Transfer to saucepan with meat and stock; add sweet potatoes. Simmer until potatoes are almost cooked, adding cabbage and spring onions for the last few minutes. Serve broth in soup bowls and meat and vegetables separately.

CHINA

The meats, seafood and vegetables of this dish are cooked in a full-flavoured boiling stock by guests at the table. If you don't have a 'steamboat' or 'firepot' you can use an electric wok or pan. Accompany the dish with hot white rice and dipping sauces. Unless you have two cooking utensils, don't attempt serving this to more than 6 people.

STEAMBOAT DINNER
Serves 6

- 10 cups stock
- 500 g (1 lb) fillet or rump steak
- 500 g (1 lb) chicken breast fillets or lean pork fillet
- 500 g (1 lb) raw prawns
- 250 g (8 oz) fresh scallops
- 125 g (4 oz) snow peas or sugar snap peas
- 4 squares fresh bean curd
- 375 g (12 oz) Chinese vegetables
- 250g (8 oz) fresh bean sprouts
- Ginger-soy Sauce
- Chilli Sauce

STOCK Put 1 kg chicken soup pieces into a large saucepan with 3 litres cold water, 1 star anise, 6 slices fresh ginger, 1 teaspoon whole black peppercorns and 1 onion. Bring to boil and skim surface. Cover and simmer gently until reduced to about 2.5 litres. Strain and add salt to taste.

PREPARING INGREDIENTS Partially freeze meats and cut into paper-thin slices. Shell and devein prawns. Wash and clean scallops if necessary. Remove strings from snow peas. Cut bean curd into thin slices. Trim any tough pieces from broccoli sprigs. Wash bean sprouts and pinch off straggly ends. Arrange meats, seafood and vegetables on separate serving platters.

In front of each diner set out a plate, bowl, porcelain spoon, chopsticks and individual sauce dishes. Fill steamboat or other cooking container three-quarters full with hot stock. Cover and place it in centre of table; allow stock to come to boil. Place a large bowl of hot white rice on table for guests to help themselves. Guests first select meat and seafood items of choice with chopsticks and hold them in the bubbling stock for no longer than 90 seconds. It is best to cook one type of food at a time as some take longer than others—do not overcook. These items are then dipped in sauce of choice. When meats and seafood have been consumed, add vegetables and bean curd to broth. Cover and simmer for a few minutes, then ladle soup into individual bowls.

GINGER-SOY SAUCE Combine 2 teaspoons finely grated fresh ginger, ¼ cup Japanese soy sauce, 2 tablespoons each sherry and water, 2 teaspoons sugar and 1 teaspoon sesame oil.

CHILLI SAUCE Choose a sweet or medium hot bottled chilli sauce.

Put a little of each sauce into individual sauce dishes.

KOREA

STIR-FRIED COMBINATION WITH BEEF
Serves 4

- 375 g (12 oz) beef fillet or rump
- 1 teaspoon sugar
- 1 tablespoon soy sauce
- 1 tablespoon finely chopped spring onion
- 2 cloves garlic, crushed
- 1 teaspoon toasted, ground sesame seeds
- ¼ teaspoon ground black pepper
- 1 tablespoon sesame oil
- 60 g (2 oz) bean thread vermicelli
- 125 g (4 oz) white Chinese cabbage, shredded
- 2 eggs, separated
- oil for stir-frying
- 2 medium-size carrots, cut into julienne strips
- 1 cup sliced bamboo shoots
- 1 medium-size onion, sliced finely
- 2 small seedless cucumbers, sliced into strips
- 1 bunch spinach, trimmed, washed and shredded
- soy sauce, sugar, salt and pepper to taste

Cut beef into paper-thin strips (this is easier if beef is partially frozen). Place in a bowl with sugar, soy sauce, spring onion, garlic, sesame seeds, black pepper and sesame oil. Stir and leave to marinate for 30 minutes. Cook noodles in boiling water for 5 minutes, then drain and cut into 7 cm (3 inch) lengths. Cook egg yolks into a flat omelette, remove to a plate; cook egg whites similarly. Cut into shreds.

Heat a wok and use just enough oil to stir-fry the meat and each vegetable separately, very quickly, over high heat. As each one is cooked, remove to a large bowl or serving dish. Toss and season with soy sauce, sugar, salt and pepper. Serve hot.

What makes this special is the marinade, using typical Korean flavours.

Barbecued Beef Ribs
Serves 4 to 6

- *1.5 kg (3 lb) beef short ribs*
- *½ cup soy sauce*
- *1 tablespoon sesame oil*
- *1 tablespoon honey*
- *2 tablespoons toasted, crushed sesame seeds*
- *¼ cup finely chopped spring onion*
- *½ teaspoon ground black pepper*
- *2 teaspoons finely grated fresh ginger*
- *2 teaspoons crushed garlic*

Have short ribs cut into short lengths and slit meat so flavours penetrate. Combine remaining ingredients and pour over meat. Cover and marinate for 4 hours, turning frequently. Cook over glowing coals or under griller, turning until meat is browned and crisp on all sides. Ribs are picked up in the fingers to eat. Serve with steamed white rice.

Various fillings are rolled inside pancakes, then dipped in sauce before eating.

NINE VARIETIES
Serves 4

PANCAKES
- *1½ cups plain flour*
- *¼ teaspoon salt*
- *3 eggs, beaten*
- *1 cup milk*
- *vegetable oil for frying*

FILLING
- *10 dried shiitake (Chinese) mushrooms*
- *soy sauce*
- *sugar*
- *black pepper*
- *vegetable oil or sesame oil or a mixture of the two*
- *4 eggs, separated*
- *375 g (12 oz) fillet of beef*
- *3 tender carrots*
- *12 spring onions*
- *1 giant white radish*
- *500 g (1 lb) zucchini*

Dipping Sauce

- *½ cup soy sauce*
- *3 tablespoons rice or white wine vinegar*
- *3 tablespoons crushed, toasted sesame seeds*
- *2 tablespoons finely chopped spring onions*
- *1 tablespoon sugar*

Pancakes Sift flour and salt into a bowl. Mix beaten eggs with milk and 1½ cups water, add to flour and beat until smooth. Let batter stand while preparing Filling. (Alternatively you can make the batter in a food processor.)

Heat a small frying or crepe pan, grease it very lightly with oil and make thin, small pancakes. Pile in centre of a tray.

Filling Soak dried mushrooms in hot water for 30 minutes. Squeeze water from mushrooms, reserving 1 cup water. Discard stems and slice caps into thin shreds. Put into pan with soaking water, 2 tablespoons soy sauce, 2 teaspoons sugar, pinch of pepper and 1 teaspoon sesame oil. Cover and cook for 20 minutes or until mushrooms are tender and liquid absorbed.

Beat egg yolks and egg whites separately and cook in a lightly greased frying pan to make one yellow and one white sheet of egg without browning. Cool and slice into fine strips.

Shred beef very finely (you will find this easier if meat is partially frozen). Heat about 1½ tablespoons of oil in a pan and stir-fry beef, adding soy sauce and black pepper to taste. Shred vegetables finely and stir-fry each separately for only a short time to retain their natural colours. Arrange Filling ingredients in separate piles around pancakes on a tray.

Dipping Sauce Blend ingredients and divide into individual sauce bowls.

JAPAN

A very good idea for family meals—soup, rice and chicken all in one dish. Children especially love it.

RICE WITH FRIED CHICKEN
Serves 6

- *1 small roasting chicken or 750 g (1½ lb) chicken fillets*
- *½ cup bottled teriyaki sauce*
- *¼ cup mirin or dry sherry*
- *500 g (1 lb) short grain rice*
- *¼ cup oil*
- *2 or 3 spring onions, chopped finely*
- *3 cups strong chicken stock*
- *3 teaspoons sugar*

Cut chicken into joints (save back and neck for stock) or fillets into pieces. Marinate chicken in teriyaki and sherry for 1 hour. Cook rice in 3 cups water, bring to boil, lower heat, cover and steam for 15 minutes. While rice steams, heat oil in heavy pan, drain chicken from marinade and fry till golden brown. Arrange on rice in serving bowl. Heat stock with reserved marinade and sugar. Stir in spring onions, pour over rice and chicken. Serve hot.

If you have the appropriate gas cooker or electric frying pan you can cook this traditional one-pot meal at the table. Accompany it with bowls of hot white rice. It is customary for each diner to break an egg in a bowl, beat it lightly with chopsticks and then dip the freshly cooked hot food into it before eating.

SUKIYAKI

- *1 kg (2 lb) fillet, scotch fillet or rump steak in one piece*
- *6 dried shiitake (Chinese) mushrooms*
- *12 spring onions*
- *1 small can winter bamboo shoots*
- *2 tender carrots*
- *2 medium onions*
- *250 g (8 oz) fresh bean sprouts*
- *1 small white Chinese cabbage*
- *60 g (2 oz) bean thread vermicelli*
- *6 pieces tofu (bean curd)*
- *piece of beef suet or vegetable oil for frying*
- *Japanese soy sauce*
- *sugar*
- *sake or dry sherry*
- *beef stock*
- *6 eggs, optional*

Freeze steak for about an hour or until just firm enough to cut into very thin slices. Soak mushrooms in hot water for

30 minutes. Wash and trim spring onions and slice into bite-size pieces, including green portion. Drain bamboo shoots and slice thinly. Peel carrots and cut into julienne strips. Peel onions and cut lengthwise into eighths. Wash bean sprouts and remove any straggly tails. Wash cabbage and cut into bite-size pieces, discarding any tough leaves. Cook noodles in boiling water for 10 minutes, then drain and cut into short lengths.

Squeeze water from soaked mushrooms, discard stems and cut caps into slices. Arrange ingredients on a platter.

Heat a heavy frying pan and rub with beef suet. Or heat just enough oil to film base of pan. Add half of each vegetable to pan and fry over high heat for 1 to 2 minutes, or until tender but still crisp. Push to one side of pan and add slices of meat in one layer. When cooked on one side, turn to cook the other (it will not take long since the meat is so thin). Sprinkle meat and vegetables with soy sauce, sugar and sake to taste, adding a little stock to moisten. Mix in noodles and tofu; heat through. Serve immediately—guests help themselves from the pan.

After the first batch has been consumed, more ingredients are added to the pan and cooked. Add more stock, soy sauce, sake and sugar and simmer as required.

Paper-thin slices of meat and vegetables are dipped with chopsticks first into a boiling stock, and then into a Sesame Seed Sauce. The dish is eaten with rice and once all the steak and vegetables are consumed the stock is served as a soup. This is not taken with a spoon but drunk direct from bowls.

SIMMERED STEAK AND VEGETABLES
Serves 6 to 8

- *1 kg (2 lb) fillet or rump steak, in one piece*
- *1 small white Chinese cabbage*
- *2 leeks*
- *2 carrots*
- *375 g (12 oz) button mushrooms*
- *1 block tofu*
- *8 to 10 cups chicken stock*

SESAME SEED SAUCE
- *⅓ cup sesame seeds*
- *2 tablespoons rice vinegar or white wine vinegar*
- *¾ cup Japanese soy sauce*
- *3 tablespoons finely chopped spring onion*
- *1 teaspoon finely grated fresh ginger*
- *1 teaspoon sugar*

Cut steak into very thin slices. (This is easier if meat is partially frozen.) Cut cabbage into short lengths. Wash leeks thoroughly to remove any grit and slice diagonally into bite-size pieces. Peel carrots and cut across in diagonal slices. Trim ends from mushrooms and wipe caps with paper towel. Cut tofu into squares. Arrange prepared food on a serving platter; cover and refrigerate until ready to serve.

If you have a shabu-shabu cooker or similar, pour stock into it. Alternatively use a table-top cooker or electric pan. Heat stock and place cooker in centre of table. Keep stock simmering throughout meal and add more if necessary.

Place a bowl, chopsticks and sauce dish at each setting. Set a large bowl of hot white rice on the table so that guests can serve themselves. Ingredients are picked from the serving platter with chopsticks and held in the boiling stock until just done, then transferred to individual bowls. Make sure that steak and vegetables are not overcooked. The meat should be pale pink and the vegetables tender but still crisp.

SESAME SEED SAUCE   Toast sesame seeds in a small dry pan over moderate heat, stirring constantly, for about 5 minutes. Turn onto a plate to cool and then crush with a mortar and pestle. Mix with remaining ingredients, stirring until sugar dissolves. (The sauce can also be combined in a blender.)

GLOSSARY

Most of these ingredients are found in Asian stores though many have made their way into supermarkets.

ANNATTO SEEDS   Used for colouring and flavouring Filipino food. Also known as achuete (pronounced ash-way-tay).

BAMBOO SHOOTS   Purchase in cans. Winter bamboo shoots are smaller and more tender than large bamboo shoots.

BASMATI RICE   Sold in Indian grocers and some supermarkets. Easy to cook but requires washing. Leave 30 minutes in colander to drain and dry.

BEAN CURD   Made from soy beans and high in protein, it is available fresh in various forms—soft, firm, fried, or in tetra packs.

BEAN THREAD VERMICELLI   Transparent noodles made from mung beans.

BLACK BEANS   Salted, fermented soy beans sold in cans or packets. Rinse away excess salt and use as recipe suggests.

CARDAMOM   Large black pods or small green pods. Use the latter. If ground cardamom is required, open pods and with mortar and pestle pound the small brown or black seeds inside. In some recipes the whole pod is used, bruised slightly to release fragrance.

CHILLIES   Small chillies are hotter than large ones. Fresh chillies should be handled with care as the volatile oils can cause much discomfort. Wear gloves especially when chopping. Substitute chopped chillies in jars, sambal ulek or Tabasco sauce.

CINNAMON   Most ground cinnamon is cassia, which is not as delicate. Be watchful when buying cinnamon quills as I have seen the thick, dark bark of cassia also labelled cinnamon. True cinnamon quills have many layers of fine, pale brown bark.

CLOVES   Can be overpowering, so don't use more than the stated amount.

CEYLON CURRY POWDER   A dark roasted blend distinctly different from supermarket curry powder, though many of the same spices are included. Sold in specialty food stores.

COCONUT MILK   Some brands of canned coconut milk are thick and rich, others very thin. The former should be diluted with water in equal parts, the latter used straight.

CORIANDER   Coriander seeds and fresh coriander are different in flavour and usage. Dried ground coriander seeds are one of the main ingredients in curries. Fresh coriander herb is essential in Thai and Chinese cooking.

CURRY LEAVES (MURRAYA KOENIGII)   Some shops sell fresh curry leaves and some nurseries sell little plants. Also available dried.

DRIED SHRIMP PASTE   (Blachan) Used in minute quantities to bring out flavours in food. Keeps indefinitely. Store in a screwtop jar to confine the smell.

FISH SAUCE   A thin, salty sauce used in South-East Asian food.

FIVE SPICE POWDER   A combination of ground star anise, fennel, cinnamon, cloves and Szechwan pepper.

GALANGAL, GREATER (ALPINIA GALANGA)   Also called laos, lengkuas and kha. Similar in size and appearance to ginger but with different flavour. Sold in large slices pickled in brine which keeps indefinitely in the refrigerator. Also sold as dried slices or powder.

GALANGAL, LESSER (ALPINIA OFFICINARUM)   Also called aromatic ginger, kencur, zeodary or krachai. Smaller in size but stronger in flavour, it is used less often than greater galangal. Sold bottled in brine in fine strips, or dried and powdered.

GARAM MASALA   Essential in Indian dishes. The commercial varieties are never as good. Roast separately until fragrant 2 tablespoons coriander seeds, 1 tablespoon cummin seeds, 2 teaspoons whole black peppercorns, 1 teaspoon cardamom seeds (remove from pods), 2 cinnamon sticks and 10 whole cloves. Grind as finely as possible and mix in half a nutmeg, finely grated. Store airtight.

GHEE   Clarified butter, sold in tins. Can be heated to a higher temperature because it has no milk solids which will burn.

GINGER   Fresh ginger root is sold at most greengrocers. Dried ground ginger should not be substituted.

KAFFIR LIME LEAVES   Essential in Thai cooking—fresh, frozen and dried.

KALONJI SEEDS (NIGELLA)   Sometimes called black cummin though not a member of the cummin family. No substitute. Mostly from Indian shops.

LEMON GRASS   Use the white or pale green tender portion of the stem. Substitute 2 strips thinly peeled lemon rind for each stem of lemon grass.

MOONG DHAL   Mung or moong beans are used as a lentil after being dried, skinned and split.

OYSTER SAUCE   A thick sauce for Chinese food.

PALM SUGAR   Has a distinct flavour but may be substituted by brown sugar.

RICE NOODLES   See page 32.

ROTI FLOUR   Also called Sharps. Slightly granular, similar to Continental flour which may be substituted.

SAFFRON   Beware of imitations as nothing else has the same flavour. Expensive, but very little is needed. Keeps well if stored airtight. Sold in strands (best to buy these) or tiny packets of powder. Distrust cheap saffron—there is no such thing.

SAMBAL ULEK (OELEK)   See **Chillies**.

SESAME OIL   Use Oriental sesame oil made from roasted sesame which is dark in colour and very aromatic. Light coloured sesame oil (usually sold in health food stores) will not impart the same flavour.

SILVER LEAF (EDIBLE)   Real silver is beaten incredibly thin and used to decorate special festive dishes. Purchase from Indian shops where it will be called Varak or from art suppliers, but make sure it is pure silver. It will be interleaved with sheets of tissue. Flutter onto the food, holding the tissue sheets with completely dry hands. No substitute.

SOY SAUCE   Dark soy (thick, coloured with caramel); light soy (thin, salty); and Japanese soy (shoyu). For best results, use the specified kind.

STAR ANISE   Dried, star-shaped seed pod imparts flavour to Chinese food. Simmered in long-cooked dishes.

SZECHWAN PEPPER   Not hot in the conventional sense, but gives a numbing sensation on the tongue. Roast over low heat to make them aromatic, and crush to powder.

TAMARIND   Imparts acidity to many dishes. *Ripe* tamarind is sold dried, pureed or in 'instant' form. The dried pulp has the truest flavour. Soak in hot water, dissolve pulp, strain. Some tamarind concentrate is very acidic, so go easy. *Green* tamarind is sold in jars in a briny liquid and gives the correct sour flavour of Filipino food.

TOFU   Japanese style fresh bean curd. Readily available in tetra packs in Asian shops and health food stores.

TURMERIC   A tropical rhizome, most readily available as a yellow powder used to flavour and colour pickles, rice and curries.

YAM BEAN OR SWEET TURNIP   In Mexico this is called jicama. In Asian shops ask for saa gott or bangkwang. A pale brown, minaret-shaped underground tuber with crisp, sweet flesh like water chestnuts. Use in salads, relishes and lightly cooked dishes.

INDEX